Iliana,
I hope the book
for you. Enjoy!

Marty

THAT'S
YOUR
BUSINESS

The Lost Virtue of
Personal Responsibility

MARTY FUQUA

Published by Best Seller Publishing®, Pasadena, California
Best Seller Publishing® is a registered trademark
Printed in the United States of America.

ISBN: 978-1-708137-69-4

This publication is designed to provide accurate and authoritative information with regard to the subject matter covered. It is sold with the understanding that the publisher is not engaged in rendering legal, accounting, or other professional advice. If legal advice or other expert assistance is required, the services of a competent professional should be sought. The opinions expressed by the authors in this book are not endorsed by Best Seller Publishing® and are the sole responsibility of the author rendering the opinion.

Most Best Seller Publishing® titles are available at special quantity discounts for bulk purchases for sales promotions, premiums, fundraising, and educational use. Special versions or book excerpts can also be created to fit specific needs.

For more information, please write:
Best Seller Publishing®
1346 Walnut Street, #205
Pasadena, CA 91106
Or call: 1 (626) 765-9750
Toll-free: 1(844) 850-3500
Visit us online at: www.BestSellerPublishing.org

Contents

Introduction

I have been in the Christian ministry for over forty years. During those years, I've counseled people from their teens to their senior years, women and men, wealthy and poor, the very gifted to the "salt of the earth." I have learned that people can be wonderful, and they can be terrible. The potential for good and for bad lives in each of us. We all have fortunate and unfortunate events happen in our lives. What is it, then, that separates those who seem to thrive from those who merely survive?

I believe learning to take personal responsibility for your life is crucial in every successful and well-adjusted person. It has become obvious to me that many of the elements of happiness and success are rooted in taking personal responsibility. Living life as a victim of others or "the system" only leads to self-pity and bitterness.

I have written this book as an inspiration for you to take personal responsibility for your life. For years, people in my life have encouraged me to write a book that included what they called "Marty-isms." These are sayings that people have heard me use in sermons, classes, and personal conversations. It is fair to say that these quips have flavored my communication for all of my professional life. I have to be honest in that the majority of these sayings did not originate with me. They are a compilation of things said to me by my parents, coaches, teachers, friends, and mentors. The truth is, these idioms are not original to them either. Rather, they are "common sense" expressions passed on from generation to generation. These sayings often are blunt and a bit "in your face." They can also seem simplistic and old-fashioned. Most of them address real-life situations which nearly everyone finds themselves in from time to time.

In large part, this real-life struggle for many of us has compelled me to write this book. My observation is that our society is progressively abandoning the conviction that each individual is responsible for his or her own words, actions, and the outcome of their life. I wholeheartedly believe we must each learn to take responsibility for our own lives. In addition, it is undeniable that we need other people. My earliest remembrances are of things my parents would say and repeat to me growing up. So much of the foundation of good thinking and good decision-making starts at home. When I began attending school, my circle of influencers grew to include teachers and eventually coaches as well. Not every teacher was great. Not every coach had a totally positive impact on me. Learning how to manage these "not perfect" relationships in our lives is very important, and often begins at an early age.

When I became a Christian and understood the Bible as a book that teaches us how to live, it became the primary influence upon my moral convictions and a practical guide for managing my life. Common sense and wise words appear throughout the Bible. The Old Testament books of Psalms, Proverbs, and Ecclesiastes are all in the part of the text known as "wisdom literature" for a reason. The foundation of every individual's life centers around the answers to these questions: Who are you? What do you believe? What will *you* do? What will *you* overcome? This emphasis on self should not be interpreted as selfishness. In fact, in most cases, if people learn to take care of their own lives, they will develop the character and concern that leads to selflessness and the ability to help others. While many people may long to serve others in need, their own lives are so out of control that they end up consumed with and focusing on their own problems. They become unable to help others. The good news is that you do not have to be bogged down with overwhelming life choices. You can get yourself together. You can make real progress. You can value the simple lessons that will push you in the right direction. It will be challenging, demanding sacrifice and endurance. It *can* be done! Let's get started on a lifetime journey of personal responsibility because, as we know, "That's your business!"

Prologue

While a student at Eastern Illinois University, I had come home for the summer break. One night I was out with friends drinking beer and driving the country roads around my hometown of Geneseo, Illinois. We passed over Interstate 80 just outside of town and thought it would be an awesome idea to urinate on the cars and trucks passing below. "They can't do anything about it," we thought. "After all, we are out in the farmland, and they are going 70 mph on the interstate." What we didn't figure into the equation was that the trucks were equipped with CB (citizens band) radios which allowed the drivers to communicate with each other. Unfortunately, CB operators could also be overheard by the area police. The local authorities were waiting for us to come back into town, and I was promptly arrested for disorderly conduct. No alcohol-related charges were made because a couple of the guys with me were important players on our local football team and they needed to have clean records in order to play that Fall.

Now I had a real dilemma. Should I tell my parents or hope they wouldn't find out about it? I worried that the local newspaper would print this in its weekly edition of the police report which included names and descriptions of all those arrested in the area.

I reasoned that it would be better for me to go ahead and tell Mom and Dad instead of having to endure their shock when they saw the report in the paper. So, I worked up my courage and went to my dad and told him what I had done. I don't remember what he said, but I do remember he didn't get angry and I did not get a lecture. However, I will never forget what happened next! I asked him if he would talk to the newspaper editor to ask if he could keep the report out of the paper. He said, "Son, that's YOUR business" and walked away. It hit me like a slap in the face. He wasn't concerned about his reputation or people's reactions. He was primarily concerned with not rescuing me from the consequences which my foolish decision would bring. It was direct. It was blunt. It was clear. It said, "Marty, you are old enough to have better judgment than this. You are old enough to stand alone and take personal responsibility for your actions, good and bad." It was a pivotal moment in my life.

It wasn't the first and surely not the last time that my dad said something to me that really struck a chord, but this lesson has continued to resonate with me through the years. Whenever I have had to make important decisions in my life, I would be reminded of this moment. Should I go into the ministry? That's your business. Should I marry Chris? That's your business. Should I sell almost everything I had and go on the mission in Buenos Aires, Argentina? That's your business. Should I adopt a young Russian girl? That's your business. I'm quite sure my dad did not always agree with all of the choices that I made, but I never heard about it. He believed in a grown man taking responsibility for his own decisions. I have come to appreciate his confidence that I would work things out on my own eventually.

Taking personal responsibility for your life is becoming a lost virtue. We live in a time when people are "victims" of almost everything. Their parents, teachers, coaches, race, gender, economic standing, and many other influences and circumstances are the imagined reasons for their failures. Instead of being overcomers, they live lives with a ready excuse that dooms them to continue being the victim. We can do better. We must do better! Let's dive into the deep end of the pool, take a good look at ourselves, and make some progress in our lives. This leads us to a favorite Marty-ism: "Improvement is always appreciated." More on that later.

By the way—the report of my malfeasance never appeared in the local newspaper.

CHAPTER 1

Core Beliefs

"If you don't stand for something, you will fall for anything"—is attributed to Alexander Hamilton and others. This chapter's **guiding principle** is that our core beliefs need to be identified, evaluated, and perhaps reinforced or changed to strengthen our foundation.

I live in earthquake country, California. In that environment, the solid foundation of any building is crucial. Structures and roads are evaluated and reinforced to try to prepare for the inevitable seismic event. Yet when it hits, the property will be destroyed and lives will be lost because of weak foundations that could not withstand the stress of such a disaster. Jesus spoke of a similar event in the book of Matthew 7:24-27, "everyone who hears these words of mine and puts them into practice is like a wise man who builds his house on the rock. The rain came down, the streams rose, and the winds blew and beat against that house; yet, it did not fall, because it had its foundation on the rock. But everyone who hears these words of mine and does not put them into practice is like a foolish man who built his house on the sand. The rain came down, the streams rose, and the winds blew and beat against that house, and it fell with a great crash." The foundation of our lives is made up of the deeply held beliefs that we use as the beginning point upon which we make decisions. Everyone has them, although they may be quite different from person-to-person. Whether a part of your conscious thought processes, they are present and comprise your personal foundation. The question that all of us have to ask ourselves is: Will my core convictions stand up to the "storms of life" that everyone will face? We do not know when or how, but everyone will be tested by the challenges of life. Your earthquake is coming!

Taking responsibility for your life is the result of core beliefs that guide your decision-making. Let's examine three of mine.

Number One
My life is a gift, and I am responsible for it.

I have always believed that I was a very blessed person. I remember as a small boy thinking how sweet it was that my dad was a school administrator and coach. We could go to the school gym almost any time because my dad had the keys! I could climb the rope, play on the pegboard, shoot baskets, and basically run and play like the prince of a kingdom. I was often lazy in my schoolwork because I believed it would all work out, and I would get into college. I thought that my parents were great parents (most of the time), that my hometown was a great place to live, etc. This feeling that your life is a special and precious gift is actually an important aspect of life, not only personal responsibility, but also, of a healthy faith in God. King David made several comments in his writings about his feelings in this regard. In Psalm 139:14, he writes, "I praise you because I am fearfully and wonderfully made." Psalm 16:5-6 continues, "Lord, you have assigned me my portion and my cup; You have made my lot secure. The boundary lines have fallen for me in pleasant places; surely I have a delightful inheritance." What a positive perspective he had about his life! In Psalm 18:50, David says, "He gives his king great victories; he shows unfailing kindness to his anointed, to David and his descendants forever."

Many have heard the popular saying, "With great blessing comes great responsibility." That has roots in many Bible stories, certainly in the story of David. You might be thinking to yourself, "Well, Marty, that's fine for you, but my life isn't like yours. My family life wasn't great. The neighborhood I grew up in wasn't great. I've had to struggle for everything I've ever had." I believe absolutely every person is created by God and is on Earth for his glory to be demonstrated through their lives. Taking responsibility for your life is rooted in the trust that God has given you exactly what you need in your life.

Every life is unique, with infinite numbers of possible influences and outcomes. Nobody's life will be the same as someone else's. If your early life was full of hardship and struggle and you have kept a positive attitude, then you have probably developed a toughness and endurance that sometimes are sadly lacking in those who have had an easy early life. If your early life was hard, and you became bitter and resentful, then it is probably easy to blame your feelings on others. The key to this whole concept is to deeply believe that God is your father, and he "set you up" to live a life that will bring about his glory.

For many, God himself is first on the list to blame for your life not turning out the way you would like it to.

Why am I not smarter? Why did my parents' marriage end in divorce? Why am I not more attractive? Why was my family not like my friend's family? Why don't I have a lot of money? And on and on it goes. People are born into all kinds of situations, and some are almost unimaginably bad. Still, you were made by God to reflect his glory. This is, at times, a very difficult concept to accept. Yet, the world is full of people who have come from terrible situations and yet have made great decisions, have persevered, and have not only lived full lives but have also been a tremendous inspiration to others around them. They are the overcomers, the heroes, and the role models we look to for inspiration during troublesome times in our lives. Let me mention a few historical examples.

Helen Keller was born in 1880. She was rendered deaf and blind by disease as a toddler. In spite of those life challenges, she rose to be a noted author, lecturer, and fought for women's rights. She serves as a tremendous inspiration to those who are deaf or blind, exemplifying that they can communicate and thrive in the world. Likewise, for those who can see and hear, she represents the great qualities of hard work, grit, and perseverance when things get hard. She was mentored by her teacher Anne Sullivan and in doing so also serves as an example of humility. Her life has made a lasting impact on the world.

Helen Keller was exceptional in attitude and actions. She was an advocate and activist for the blind and deaf and for women's rights. Here she is at the White House with President John F. Kennedy (1961) and her translator who communicated with her through hand taps.

Credit: Alamy Photos

President Franklin Roosevelt was born into wealth, education, and a life of ease. Stricken with paralysis at age 39, he lost the use of both of his legs. In spite of his disability, he persevered and led an extraordinary life of public service. He was elected governor of New York and later elected four times to the presidency of the United States. He was noted for his positive attitude toward life in spite of his obvious personal struggles. While he relied on support from leg braces and assistants for public appearances, in private he was confined to a wheelchair. Most Americans of the time had no idea their president was unable to walk unassisted. What a great example we see in his famous quote: "Men are not prisoners of fate, but only prisoners of their own minds."

FDR campaigning from the back of his train.

He is standing with the help of leg braces leaning on his son, James.
He did not allow his challenges to limit what he could do.

Credit: Alamy Photos

Anthony Robles was an American amateur wrestler. While he may not be as well-known as my first two examples, he is notable for taking the life he was given and making the most of it. For reasons unknown, Anthony was born into this world with only one leg. He struggled throughout his young life, but because of his disability, he developed a very strong upper body, eventually setting the push-up record at his school. Anthony took up wrestling after watching one of his cousin's practices. He enjoyed minimal success at first. His record as a freshman in high school was five wins and eight losses. He was ranked last in his weight class in his hometown of Mesa, Arizona. By his junior and senior years, he built a record of 96 wins and zero losses and won the state championship. He learned to take advantage of his incredibly strong grip (as a result of being on crutches all his life) and some crafty moves that only a one-legged wrestler could pull off. He earned a wrestling scholarship to Arizona State University and in his senior year won a national championship. Not bad for a boy with one leg! He learned not to focus on what he lacked, but rather on what he *did* have. This ended up being a fabulous strategy for success.

All three of these great individuals undoubtedly struggled with feeling overwhelmed and at times frustrated with a perceived lack of progress. They had to ask as we all do in times of struggle, "Why is my life so hard?" The answer is that all lives are challenging at times. Yes, some are harder, but all lives have unique difficulty. Jesus said it well in Matthew 6:34, "each day has enough trouble of its own." The following is a two-fold truth: Life is a gift, *and* life is hard. God has granted me the ability to be grateful, to be happy, and to improve—to become a better individual. Conversely, I can become angry, impatient, and bitter when I face difficulty and disappointment. Here is what we all have to believe if we are to make progress in our lives: "It's my choice. It's my life. It's my business!"

Anthony Robles declared national champion. An amazing example of grit and creativity.

Source: Journalstar.com

Number Two
I am capable of making good and bad decisions.

Part of taking responsibility for your life is humbly admitting that you have made both good and bad decisions. Our acceptance of this principle can influence our ability to take responsibility for our lives. An interesting phenomenon can occur when we make good decisions that work out well for us. We can tend to feel pleased with ourselves and start to believe that we are pretty smart. We take full credit for our good decisions. Conversely, when we make a bad decision, we tend not to rush to take responsibility for it. We start looking around, searching for the person responsible for this mess. One of my very best friends, Bob Harpole, said something to me that was blunt, but true, several years ago. During one of our usual golf outings, I hit a shot far into the rough instead of on the green, where I had aimed. I moaned about what a bad lie I had, how the ball was sitting very low in the tall grass, and how it was unfair that the grounds crew didn't do a better job preparing the course for play. With neither emotion nor eye contact, Bob replied, "Well, I guess you shouldn't have hit the ball there." I was stunned, but I had to admit he was absolutely right. He didn't baby me; he didn't blame the course or the grounds crew. I had made a poor shot, and the position of the ball was my own fault.

I have made many good golf shots over the years. When I hit a good one, I don't start thinking of all the people who made my clubs, cut the grass, or designed the course. I take full credit that I hit a darn good shot. But when I hit a bad one, I can moan and gripe and get angry. Blaming others doesn't fix the problem or help me to be honest with myself about what happened. It doesn't motivate me to learn how to improve next time. We all need trusted people in our lives that love us enough to tell us what we need to hear and what we often don't want to hear. Bob had just spoken the truth, and I decided to trust him. I was able to learn from my mistake. Now, anytime someone in our golf group starts to gripe about a bad shot they made, someone else usually says, "I guess you shouldn't have hit it there." These types of sayings can become a touchstone in your personal culture and can remind you to embrace new opportunities to learn a better way.

This is my life and my business, and I must take responsibility for my decisions. How can I learn wisdom and the art of making good choices? The scriptures indicate that when we seek God's guidance, we can make good decisions. Here are some thoughts and biblical verses to help us along this path.

- Seek guidance from God. Psalm 143:8 says, "Show me the way I should go, for to you, I lift up my soul."
- Get advice from trusted spiritual friends. Proverbs 20:18 instructs us to "make plans by seeking advice."
- Ask God to bless you with greater wisdom. James 1:5 tells us, "If any of you lacks wisdom, you should ask God, who gives generously to all without finding fault, and it will be given to you."

What about our bad decisions? Do they mean we are doomed to ruin our lives? I believe that just as any parent knows that their children will not always make good decisions, our heavenly father also knows that we will make poor choices at times. He knows that we will periodically make mistakes in judgment, and sometimes just plain do the wrong thing. He eagerly watches our lives to see how we react when we mess up. Do we whine, blame, and sulk, or do we "man up" or "woman up" and take responsibility for our decisions and actions?

The other side of this equation is also open to the father's observation. When we make the right decisions, do we brag and puff ourselves up with narcissistic presumptions about our abilities?

It is always a good practice to be humble, to let others praise you and to thank those who helped influence that good moment. It is a mockery of humility to openly boast when we have success and then end our sharing with a disclaimer of "To God be the glory" to deflect any accusation of being boastful and full of pride. Most people see right through that type of false humility.

The scriptures are quite clear how we need to conduct ourselves.

- Proverbs 30:32 says, "If you play the fool and exalt yourself, clap your hand over your mouth."
- Proverbs 27:2 continues this line of thinking, "Let another praise you, and not your own mouth; someone else, and not your own lips." God clearly does not appreciate people taking personal glory!
- We find quite a gruesome story in Acts 12:21-23, "[King] Herod, wearing his royal robes, sat on his throne and delivered a public address to the people. They shouted, 'This is the voice of God, not a man.' Immediately, because Herod did not give praise to God, an angel of the Lord struck him down, and he was eaten by worms and died." Wow, what a way to go!

Here is the lesson for all of us: Be humble when you are right and be humble when you are wrong.

My wise friend, Bob Harpole.
We all need trusted advisers to
help us stay humble.

Number Three
I will not let my emotions override my convictions.

It has been said that emotions are good servants, but terrible masters. We all have emotions. In essence, our emotions help to make us who we are. Some people are more emotional than others. It is not an advantage to be one or the other. Wherever you stand in this area of life, you will need to manage your level of emotion. Jesus said that the first and greatest commandment is "Love the Lord with all of your heart and with all of your soul and with all of your mind and with all of your strength" (Mark 12:30)

We get into trouble when we start letting our emotions control us to the point that they overwhelm our convictions, wisdom, and commitment. This is not the mark of a mature person. Balancing our emotions with our convictions, though rarely easy, is what maturity demands. A conviction is a deeply held guiding principle that does not change according to circumstances. People can depend upon a person who has conviction. This type of individual is consistent, reliable, and trustworthy. Getting your emotions under control may not be the easiest way to live your life, but it is the best way to live your life. Doing or saying something because you "feel" it can get you into a lot of trouble. If we begin to live our lives governed only by feelings, we are going to do some really dangerous, hurtful and antisocial things. Unfortunately, it seems that many don't want to think as much as they want to feel. People saying and doing things out of unbridled emotion often ends in unhappiness and harm. That harm can be unintentional, but it can create damage that can last a lifetime in ours and others' lives.

Our world can be a scary place, for sure. We all worry about our physical safety, our financial security, and our personal health. Sometimes we are rightly concerned about our children, our parents, our neighbors, and ourselves. This past year, a deranged young man came to one of our outdoor church services armed with a large knife and screamed out, "Where is Marty?" as he was brandishing his weapon. He was a former member who had fallen back into drug abuse. He was angry and very confused. I was in a small serving area, helping prepare food, and was never really in harm's way. Several brave young men tackled him and held him until the police came to detain him.

Was that frightening? Yes! Several of the children and adults who were closer to the actual event were stunned and shaken. At the same time, things happened so quickly that it was interesting to note how many were confused as to what exactly occurred and so were not really afraid at all. One first-time visitor remarked, "Wow, you have an exciting church!" (Not my preferred kind of "excitement".) When things like this take place, we can tend to react and sometimes overreact. Taking prudent measures to keep ourselves and our loved ones safe is a normal and needed response, especially in our current world where evil people are a legitimate threat. Yet, we can start to imagine danger at every turn and become withdrawn and fearful of others. We need to periodically take stock and recenter ourselves onto the foundation of our core convictions. We will all confront frightening circumstances and must make sure that our fears, real or imagined, are not ruling our lives.

When I was a young boy, I went with my family to visit my uncle J.D. Guerin at his farm. He had several horses, and I was fascinated by them. They were beautiful, fast, and as I was a "town boy," something that I knew nothing about. Being ignorant of danger doesn't make the danger any less real. We were in the barn, and I started to walk closely behind the horses as they stood in their stalls. Suddenly, my uncle grabbed me by the arm and jerked me back and said curtly, "Don't walk behind a horse that doesn't know you. They will kick you and hurt you bad." I was really taken aback by how fast and hard he had grabbed me. I didn't know I was doing anything wrong or dangerous, but I could have actually gotten seriously hurt by those beautiful horses. I have never looked at a horse the same way again.

Our whole array of emotions comes into play when we are talking about taking personal responsibility for our lives in the face of fear. All areas of our life, from our family life to our professional life, involve other people. It doesn't take long until the drama begins sometimes. Feelings get hurt, leading to misunderstandings and miscommunication. "What did he mean by that?" "Why did she do that?" "I can't believe he is that big of an idiot!" On and on it goes. Before long, we are agitated, involved, taking sides, gossiping, and slandering. We are angry and hurt and, more than likely, overflowing with emotions. We start doing and saying things that are not helpful and can be downright sinful. Where did this start? Fear and emotion.

"Be a part of the solution—not a part of the problem" is one of my favorite Marty-isms. It is an axiom that compels us to think, slow down, plan a strategy, and not react to everything said around us. Try to remember; there are some battles that are not worth winning. When it comes to human relationships, sometimes the best thing to say is nothing. You don't always have to have an answer or a great comeback when in the midst of an emotion-filled exchange with your spouse, child, parent, friend, neighbor, employee, employer, fellow church member, etc. The person who feels they have to win every argument they get into is most likely a person who has left a litany of broken relationships in their wake. "Well, I know I'm right!" is what they think, and maybe say. Yes, perhaps you were right, but you have now crippled a relationship. Is that really what you wanted to do? Just like that horse from my childhood, people can hurt you. Unfortunately, some people are just mean-spirited. Many have never valued the skills necessary to de-escalate an argument. Some people are reacting to the situations they face in their lives with very few, if any, real core convictions. They may be selfish, prideful, poor communicators who must be "handled with care" lest they hurt you and those you love. I believe that is why the scriptures say things like, "keep away from them" (Romans 16:17) and "avoid anyone who talks too much" (Proverbs 20:19.)

It may be a revelation that there are different levels of friendship in life. It is perfectly normal to have people that are acquaintances who will never be your best friends. I remember several people over the years who wanted to have a closer relationship with me. Some of them even insisted that they should be my "best friend." Those precious relationships in your "inner circle" are reserved for those who through time and circumstances have proven their love for you and who value your interests in addition to their own. Who you choose as your closest friends can be one of the most valuable lessons that we learn in our own lives and then intentionally teach to our children and others. We will discuss more on this subject later.

There certainly are other convictions that are involved in taking responsibility for your life, but these three have been important to me. (1) My life is a gift, and I am responsible for it. (2) I am capable of making good and bad decisions. (3) I will not let my emotions override my convictions. Any endeavor in life has a greater chance to succeed if the fundamentals are right and well-engineered from the beginning. A football team will be on the right track if they block and tackle well. A student must have a good foundation in basic reading and math skills if they are to go very far in their educational life. A military operation will have a much greater chance of victory if they have well-trained soldiers and leadership. These three core convictions are attainable for anyone. They don't require great learning or a high IQ to understand them.

This is within your grasp. You *can* do this. Now, these principles aren't always easy, and you will have to dedicate and rededicate yourself to them over the span of time. Life can be a bit like driving a car down a road. If my wheels are straight and the road is straight, I can assume everything is just right. Yet, if I don't constantly adjust, re-evaluate, and correct errors, I will drive off the road and be in the ditch in no time. There will never be a better time than now to begin this journey. Start! Don't try to fix everything in your life; just fix *something*. Don't get overwhelmed or discouraged with a failure or a bad day.

Celebrate every success you have. Ready, set, go!

Guided Reflections

1. What are some of your core convictions?
2. Reflect on a decision you made at a stressful time in your life. How did you respond? How do you wish you would have responded?
3. What core conviction would you like to add to your present convictions? How do you think this new conviction would affect your life?

CHAPTER 2

The Missing Ingredient in Most of Us: Toughness

In this chapter, we'll discuss the **guiding principle** of inner toughness, which is an essential ingredient in the business of developing character in our lives.

I started wrestling in eighth grade with a brief two-week workshop led by our high school wrestling coach Larry Kanke and several of his wrestlers. They came down to my junior high and were introducing the sport to whoever was interested. I wasn't. My dad was a basketball player from Kentucky (serious basketball country) who had coached a junior high team from my birthplace (Cairo, Illinois) to the state tournament in Illinois. I wanted to play basketball. I did remember seeing a wrestling match earlier in Port Byron, Illinois, and one of the stars on that team was the young man who had taught the swimming class I had taken the previous summer. I wasn't very impressed. There were hardly any fans in the gym, and I had no idea what was going on. My dad, though, was looking out for his little guy. I was not very big. I was born prematurely and was much smaller than my brother my whole life.

In little league football as a fifth grader, I was the smallest player on any of the teams, weighing in at a whopping 65 pounds! I was fast and aggressive, just not physically big.

Dad said to me, "Mart, I think wrestling might be just the thing for you. You know, they didn't have wrestling in Kentucky, but if they had, I probably would have been a wrestler." That put a different light on it. I wanted to be like my dad, and it was obvious that wrestling was something he respected. It was only two weeks after all. Why not? It didn't take any time at all, and I knew I had found my sport. It was like a fight, but it also required skill. And, it was rough—I loved it immediately. They organized a little tournament at the end of the two weeks matching boys who were close in weight into four-man brackets.

I won my bracket and thought I was pretty tough. I'm giving all this background information because wrestling has had such a huge impact on my character. Wrestling is hard. Dan Gable, Olympic champion, three-time NCAA champion, and legendary coach at the University of Iowa, is quoted as saying, "After wrestling, everything is easy!" Wrestling meant long practice sessions in a hot room (to sweat even more), which led to matches against other teams with hardly any fans in the stands. Why do it? Somehow it was perfect for me. I didn't mind the hard practices or the lack of fan support. I loved the toughness that the sport required. You might be thinking, "Well, that's all good and fine for you, but that's not me. I'm a lover, not a fighter." Let me get to my point: Taking responsibility for your life requires an inner toughness that many people lack. The inner toughness required for a good wrestler, and the inner toughness required to become a responsible person are remarkably similar. It's not a "guy" thing. It's not an athlete thing. It's not an "old school" thing. It's a *heart* thing. This is something everyone can have in their life. Now, in fairness, it's harder for some to become an internally tough person than it is for others. This is true of any great heart quality. It's harder for some to be loving. It's harder for some to be kind. It's harder for some to be pure-minded. We all have an accumulation of experiences we have lived through, good and bad. We all have the DNA we inherited from our biological parents. We all have the influences of the people we have been around in our life, good and bad. This quality of unflinching tenacity is rare and seemingly becoming rarer.

Dan Gable with his gold medal from the Munich Olympics. A great Gable quote: "Wrestling, it's what the men do during boys' basketball season." Absolutely my childhood hero.
Source: Twitter.com

Here are some scriptures that touch on this subject.

- Romans 5:3-4 reads, "We also rejoice in our sufferings, because we know that suffering produces perseverance; perseverance, character; and character, hope."

- James 1:2-4 says, "Consider it pure joy, my brothers, whenever you face trials of many kinds, because you know that the testing of your faith develops perseverance. Perseverance must finish its work so that you may be mature and complete, not lacking anything."
- Galatians 6:9 instructs us, "Let us not become weary in doing good, for at the proper time we will reap a harvest if we do not give up." This inner toughness is an absolute necessity if one is to stay faithful to the Lord their entire lives.
- Shadrach, Meshach, and Abednego proclaim in Daniel 3:17-18, "If we are thrown into the blazing furnace, the God we serve is able to save us from it. But even if he does not, we want you to know, O king, that we will not serve your gods or worship the image of gold you have set up." Three unbreakable amigos!
- Esther was chosen as one of the king's wives in the Old Testament story. Esther 2:7 says of her, "This girl, who was also known as Esther, was lovely in form and features." She was also much more than a beauty queen. Her inner strength was demonstrated when her fellow Jews were threatened with genocide, and she was challenged to go to the king to defend them. In Esther 4:16 she states, "I will go to the king, even though it is against the law. And if I perish, I perish." She was willing to risk her life and security for what was right. That is one tough young lady!
- How about the early Christian church leaders when they were told by the authorities to stop speaking to others about Jesus? In Acts 4:19-20 they reply, "Judge for yourselves whether it is right in God's sight to obey you rather than God, for we cannot help speaking about what we have seen and heard." These were some seriously gritty men!

I have come to have great respect for anyone who has been a faithful Christian for many years. They have persevered. They have been around long enough to see the shortcomings and sins of their fellow Christians, yet they remain faithful to God. They have been around long enough to be disappointed by someone in a leadership position in the church. They have weathered the temptation in their own lives to leave the faith, the church, and go back to the world. They have "stuck it out" through thick and thin, and they are still faithful to the Lord and his people. Amen! They have my respect. They have persevered in spite of others' failures and even their own failures. They are "tried and true." They may be bloodied and bruised, but they did not quit because it got hard.

Perseverance is a quality that you cannot develop until you experience fatigue. Life is a marathon, not a sprint! A sprint is an explosion of energy that is over in just a few seconds. A marathon is a grueling ordeal that takes hours, even for the fastest marathoners in the world. You have all kinds of obstacles to overcome in an extremely long race. How you may feel at different points in the race is quite different. The first few miles may be great fun. Mile 23 usually is not. Seeing others around you suffering, perhaps even suffering yourself, and seeing some quit can cause you to doubt yourself. "Why am I doing this?" "I know a lot of people who aren't doing this." "I'm in pain!" (A subject I will get to later in the book.) But then, the finish line appears a few hundred yards away. All of a sudden, you feel better. Friends and family are there waiting. The band is playing, and the people are cheering you on. What a feeling to cross the finish line!

We don't know what the future holds for our own lives. We only know that for all of us, there will be hardship and times of testing. I don't think I have ever personally witnessed how a person's life could so drastically change as in the story of my friend, Jackie

Nakaishi. Jackie was one of the students in our college ministry when Chris and I were living on the west side of Los Angeles. Jackie was a student at Loyola Marymount University. She was a young woman with a solid love for God and a vibrant personality. She fell in love and married a great guy named Chris Nakaishi. They were blessed with two wonderful children, Kailee and Kevin.

Jackie Nakaishi finishing her Big Sur Marathon
after all that she had been through. Impressive!

On February 7, 2014, Jackie had just returned from a morning run when she was stricken with a terrifying pain in her head. She was not a "headache person," so she quickly realized that something was very wrong. She called her husband at work, and he told her to call 911. She was quickly transported by ambulance to the local hospital. Once there, doctors quickly ascertained that this was a situation they were not equipped to handle, so she was transported to Keck USC Medical Center. She was rushed into surgery to repair three leaking aneurysms in her brain. Over the next several months, she went through six operations: two craniotomies and four other surgical procedures to save her life. Her condition was congenital and not caused by anything she had done.

I firmly believe that God was watching over Jackie. If she had been living farther away from a world-class hospital with specially-trained surgeons, she would have likely died. She went through months of hard recovery, including physical therapy for weakness and balance problems, supported all the way by her family and friends. She was determined to get her health back in time to run the Big Sur Marathon that was scheduled for April 2015. By much-determined effort and the grace of God, she ran her race. I can tell you from personal observation; she is one tough woman! She has my respect! She is the picture of the "Never Give Up" spirit. I think it is important in our world today for people to develop an inner toughness that will sustain them in a tough world.

Indulge me a bit and let me share with you about some of the women in the Fuqua family. My daughter Maria played defense on her high school soccer team. One year, they won a CIF (California Interscholastic Federation) state championship. She was not the fastest nor the most skillful player on the team, but she was clearly one of the toughest. When the forwards on the opposing team got the ball in her part of the field, they were likely to get hit, knocked down, or lose the ball to Maria. She even kept track of how many times she did this. The opposing players remembered that the next time they got the ball in her neighborhood. One of the things I love most about Maria is that she is one of the sweetest people I know, but there's that edge of steel she has in her character as well.

Maria, my youngest child, on her championship soccer team. Three things I like about this picture: (1) The mud on Maria's shorts. (2) The intense look on her face. (3) The seemingly frustrated demeanor of the girl on the other team behind her.

Chris and I adopted our daughter Anya from Russia, and she was almost a teenager when we brought her to our home in the United States. She spoke no English and, as we found out later, did not attend school while she was growing up in Moscow. She was far behind other classmates her age. I have often thought about how difficult that must have been for her. She came to a strange new country; did not speak the language, and she was placed in a family of well-meaning strangers. There were times of great stress for all of us as we tried to help Anya get ready for adult life in the US. We had lots of help from people like Lisa Payne, Elke Nelson, and a host of others who kept us sane and helped her make progress. Anya not only hung in there but was able to graduate with her high school class, attend community college, and support herself through employment. She now has a wonderful husband and two children of her own. One can only imagine where her life would be now if she had not developed the toughness to not quit when things were hard.

Anya, our Russian daughter, is a strong woman who would not quit. She persevered through her learning challenges. We are so proud of her.

The hub of our family wheel is my wife, Chris. She was a two-sport college athlete in volleyball and softball. When I met her at church, I was impressed with her straightforward, no-nonsense way of dealing with life. She lost her father when she was a year old and endured many years of challenging family dynamics, which helped mold her into a strong and determined person of faith. I must admit I was a bit intimidated by her at first. She has influenced many women over the years with these powerful qualities. As a mother, she certainly set an example for her daughters. She challenged Maria and Anya to think, act, react, and push forward anyway when the going got tough. Her own actions and her expectations for others are very much driven by inner convictions. Personal sacrifice and hard work are at the core of her strength.

A really nice picture of Chris and me. Wow, am I glad she married me!

After our children were grown, we became empty nesters. I must say that it was pleasant to enjoy a home environment that was a bit calmer, even with our two crazy dogs, Jack and Lucy. One day Chris came to me with a concern about one of our good friends, Margaret, who was weathering a difficult divorce. She thought it might be helpful for Maggie to live with us for a while, to help her get through this rough patch in her life. Margaret had lived with us for about a year and had made great progress in her post-divorce life. Meanwhile, other events were happening. A great lady who became a Christian in our church, Maryann Ani, died of breast cancer. She had a teenage daughter named Corina who was a junior in a high school nearby. Chris came to me saying she thought we should offer Corina the opportunity to live with us and Margaret until she was able to leave for college. Corina also thought it was a great idea and moved in. We created what we called our "Framily"—friends who love each other like family. Here is the magic that happened: Margaret really needed a "younger sister" to take care of, and Corina really needed an "older sister" to help her adjust to life without her mom. All of this good happened, in part, because of Chris's willingness to sacrifice and work hard. These women have now moved on to other challenges and victories in their own lives. They have grown in their own resilience and strength because of their experiences and hold "honorary Fuqua status" in our home.

The Fuqua "Framily." Margaret (L) and Corina (R). Two wonderful women with whom we shared our home for a season.

Let's get practical. How can YOU start to become tougher in your character? The best way to develop a spirit of toughness is to cultivate self-control. Growing spiritually and growing in self-control go hand in hand. As with any development of a deep character trait, you must be patient and realize this is not going to take place overnight. You likely will have good days and bad days, even if you are really trying hard. It certainly helps most people of faith to identify with the scriptures. In Titus 2, the apostle Paul is helping young Titus think through how to meet the needs of important groups of people in the church in Crete. In verse two, he says, "Teach the older men to be self-controlled," and in verse six, "Encourage the younger men to be self-controlled." He highlights a pretty consistent theme here, doesn't he? Then he adds, "so that they will make the teaching about God our Savior attractive."

Self-control is a key component of inner toughness, which leads to taking more responsibility for our lives. Students and their parents will be relieved when they see their children attaining better grades as a result of disciplined study habits. Physical health improves because of self-control and better life convictions, such as healthy eating and regular exercise. Employers are impressed when work is done well and on time. (Perhaps a raise is in order?) Paul goes on to say in the text referenced above that, "The grace of God has appeared to all people, and it teaches us to say no to ungodliness and worldly passions and to live self-controlled and godly lives." Galatians 5:22-23 describes the various aspects of the fruit of the Spirit, "But the fruit of the Spirit is love, joy, peace, forbearance, kindness, goodness, faithfulness, gentleness, and self-control. Against such things, there is no law." The last quality listed is self-control. The "fruit," or result, of the Spirit in the life of a child of God, should be self-control, self-discipline, and inner toughness! It starts with small things that may seem basic and simple.

Harold Pinther *1925-2012*

Coach Pinther: I knew Coach Pinther for such a short time, but his honest straightforwardness was life-changing for me. Who could have ever known that I would repeat that one thing he said to me to help so many college students?
Source: eiupanthers.com

When I was being recruited to wrestle on the team at Eastern Illinois University, their coach came to my high school to talk to me about their program. His name was Harold (Hop) Pinther. He had been there for many years and was actually my high school coach's coach when he was wrestling in college at EIU. We had a great talk, and he invited my mother and me to drive down to Charleston, Illinois, to see the campus and hopefully decide to wrestle there. We drove down several weeks later, and he showed us around. I said I was very interested, but I was concerned about the academic demands of being a wrestler and a student simultaneously. His answer was a life-changing moment for me. "Don't worry about it, Marty. A lot of dumb people graduate from college every year. Go to class and do your homework, and you will graduate." What!? Did he just call me dumb? He gave me the simplest answer I could have ever expected. In essence, he encouraged me by telling me college wasn't beyond my ability, as long as I went to class and did my homework.

Over the years, I have been involved with students at many different colleges and universities as a campus minister. At all of those schools—Northern Illinois, Northwestern, University of Chicago, University of Illinois-Chicago, UCLA, USC, Cal State LA, Pasadena City College, Caltech—this simple formula for success has worked! Whatever your school, this same equation will help you graduate to go to class and do your homework! I can't tell you how many conversations I had over the years with college students who were not doing well in their classes and who were getting poor grades. I would ask if they were going to all of their classes. Almost to a person, their answer involved a lot of words and explanations, and then we would get back to the simple question. "Are you going to all of your classes?" "But-but-but," they would continue to protest. I had one student say to me, "You went to a small state school, and you couldn't have even been accepted at this school. You don't understand my level of pressure." Let's try it again. I would insist, "Are you going to all of your classes?" "No." Well, let's start there, go to class and do your homework.

It's the simple things that make all the difference. Get yourself on a schedule, get up on time, go to bed on time, eat three good meals a day, and drink plenty of water. Get the junk out of your diet, leave the video games and cell phone off when you are doing important things. It's the little things that make all the difference! After a good day, you can say to yourself, "One in a row!" An old friend of mine, Ron Marsh, was a great golfer. He would often repeat that same phrase after hitting a good shot that had been preceded by several bad shots. I loved it because it was so positive and forward-looking. Much better than dwelling on all the bad shots he had hit. "One in a row!" He expected to have several more in the future. Excellent!

Momentum is a mysterious thing. When you have it, you feel like you will never lose it. When you don't have it, you think you will never find it. It's important to remember that, in developing this inner toughness, you are not competing with anyone else but yourself. You're not trying to show up anyone, brag about your success, or put others down because they are making slower progress than you. You are trying to be the best you that you can be. If you do this, you will more than likely be surprised at how much you can accomplish. You will reach higher, run longer and faster, live healthier, and get more done than ever before.

One of the best examples of the development of inner toughness I have witnessed is my son, Ben Fuqua. Several years ago, he and some of his college buddies were sitting around and talking about how they were getting fat and out of shape. One of them suggested they all try a local triathlon that was to be held in a few weeks. Ben had not been swimming, biking, or running in a long time. As a matter

of fact, he didn't even own a bike. So, he bought a used clunker on eBay. He completed the race and was surprised at how much he enjoyed it. He began to train and enter more short-distance triathlon events. He eventually decided to try a half-Ironman race in Austin, Texas.

Ben admiring his dad after the 1993 Western Hemisphere Marathon.

Me admiring Ben finishing his Ironman at the Ironman World Championships in Kona, Hawaii, 2016.

Source: Finisherpix

Now, just so we understand, that means he was going to swim 1.2 miles, cycle 56 miles, and then complete a 13.1 mile run. This distance is sometimes referred to as a 70.3, which is the total distance of the three disciplines combined. I was impressed with his guts! He did well in that, and then (you knew this was coming) decided to do a full Ironman race. He selected one in St. George, Utah, which consisted of a 2.4 mile swim, a 112 mile bike ride, and a grueling 26.2 mile run. He finished, and I felt so proud of him and for him. His time was immaterial. His desire to improve was growing. As the great Arnold Palmer said, "The road to success is always under construction." I thought Ben was a little crazy, but he was making progress. He qualified the next two years in a row for the Half-Ironman World Championships. He did well in both of these races, but he had some setbacks. He experienced a mechanical problem with his bike in Canada and had a physical reaction to running in high elevation in Austria.

In 2016, he qualified for the Ironman World Championship held in Kona, Hawaii. I remembered the frightening TV coverage years before where a woman racer fell down several yards from the finish line, crawled to the end, and collapsed. I was a bit afraid for my son. Fortunately, Ben's hard work and determination paid off, and he had a great race. He finished as the 10th American amateur in Kona that year. He subsequently was invited to join a prestigious men's triathlon group, Team Every Man Jack. Now, I'm telling you all of this to illustrate what can happen when a bunch of guys challenge each other to do something other than sitting around watching sports on TV and getting fat. What are *you* capable of? What adventures await you? I will promise you, if you are serious about this you will see progress in your life. Remember, "Progress is always appreciated."

In any discussion about inner toughness, it is crucial that we talk about failure. Most success stories have a backdrop of someone who failed, stuck with it, and eventually had success. I have heard it said that we learn more in our moments of failure than we do in our moments of success. I don't know if that is always true, but I can say that when I don't succeed, it does make me ask the question, "What went wrong?" This is an area of life experience that we all have to deal with. Failure is tough. It's hard. It can be excruciating! No one likes to lose. But, failure one day can lead to success the next.

I love reading about American history. In the battle of Shiloh in the Civil War, General Grant was leading the Federal forces, and Albert Sidney Johnston was the lead general for the Confederate

Army. The first day of the fight was disastrous for Grant and the Federal Army. They were caught off guard. They had very poor communication from unit to unit. They made a mess of it, to say the least. Grant fell off his horse, and the horse fell on his ankle. It didn't break, but it was badly swollen, and they had to cut his boot off as a result. That's a BAD day. In the evening after the fighting had stopped, he was standing under a tree to shield himself from hard rain and his best friend and fellow general, William Tecumseh Sherman, found him. He thought that the best course of action was probably to retreat and regroup. He said to Grant, "Well, Grant, we've had the devil's own day, haven't we?" Grant, with his cigar glowing in the darkness as he gave a quick, hard puff at it, said, "Yes. Lick them tomorrow though." And that they did. They regrouped the Union Army, pushed forward on April 7 and successfully regained the ground they had lost the day before and thus, turned certain defeat into victory. Grant's determination had proven to be a critical element.

Refusing to quit is a toughness many people lack. "Quitters never win, and winners never quit" is a motto I have borrowed from many of my former coaches. "When the going gets tough, the tough get going" is another favorite of coaches. The great Green Bay Packers' coach Vince Lombardi was quoted as saying, "Fatigue makes cowards of us all." Sometimes we are just plain tired. We are tired of the struggle of life. We are tired of the "rat race" that the professional and corporate world can be. We are tired of the drama in our families. We are tired of fighting our sinful nature in a sinful world. We are tired of feeling like the moral values we think are true and foundational for a healthy society are constantly under attack.

The story of Joseph in the book of Genesis is a great study of what appeared to be a failure but was revealed to be part of a larger plan that led to the salvation of his entire family. In Genesis 45:7,

Joseph tells his brothers, "God sent me ahead of you to preserve for you a remnant on earth and to save lives by a great deliverance." It would behoove us sometimes not to be so quick to declare failure. Down the road, we may re-evaluate and realize that what was seen as a bad thing actually turned out to be for good. Romans 8:28 reads, "In all things God works for the good of those who love him." That doesn't mean that everything that happens in the life of someone who loves the Lord is good. It means that even when it is bad, it can eventually be used to bring good into our lives.

Thank God for unanswered prayers! Sometimes God says yes, and sometimes the answer is no or silence. We have to soberly think back and ask the question that if we had won that state championship, where would our lives be today? If we had won that academic scholarship, where would we be today? If we had gotten that advancement in our career, where would our lives be today? Many of these "defeats" are the very things that humble us and lead us to see our need for help in our lives. We may have felt our need for a relationship with God partly because we realized we were not enjoying the successes we had hoped for, worked for, and prayed for. Jesus said in the Sermon on the Mount, Matthew 5:3, "Blessed are the poor in spirit, for theirs is the kingdom of heaven. Blessed are those who mourn, for they will be comforted. Blessed are the meek, for they will inherit the earth. Blessed are those who hunger and thirst for righteousness, for they will be filled." All of these rich blessings are reserved for those who are poor in spirit, those who mourn, those who are meek, and those who are hungry and thirsty for what is right. It seems that Jesus is saying that the preferred attitude to have is one of humility, not pride; one that is aware of our weaknesses, not full of ourselves. Perhaps, being motivated and driven in life truly is far better than being comfortable and complacent.

Guided Reflections

1. When you hear the word "toughness," what is your reaction and why?
2. What are three areas of self-control you need to grow in, and what would be the outcome of making progress in these areas?
3. Detail some simple steps you can take in each of the above areas.

CHAPTER 3

It's My Business—
But I Need Help!

The **guiding principle** of this chapter is that we all need other people in our lives to help us to be our best. The prototypical image of the lone cowboy riding off into the sunset or the rebel with a cause on his motorcycle is what comes to mind when we think of the rugged individualist who takes care of their own business. Nothing could be further from reality.

We need others in our lives. If you think that you don't, you are probably heading for some really hard lessons in life. It is my experience that most successful people have several mentors in their life who have molded, parented, shaped, educated, and coached them along the way. They didn't get to where they are in life by just gutting it out by themselves. Two of my best friends, Rob Kosberg and Kevin Hutto, are successful businessmen who have programs that they lead to coach other businesspeople. They also typically go to at least two coaching programs per year where they are the ones being coached. Isn't that interesting? They are still being coached while they are coaching others themselves. Sadly, for many people, their years of being coached have long since passed. The open-hearted, eager young person is now the hard-headed and hard-hearted "know it all" older person. We need both—to be coached and to coach others our entire lives.

The scriptures point this out vividly.

- Ecclesiastes 4:7-12 illustrates this, "I saw something meaningless under the sun: there was a man all alone; he had neither son nor brother. There was no end to his toil, yet his eyes were not content with his wealth. 'For whom am I toiling,' he asked, 'and why am I depriving myself of enjoyment?' This too is meaningless, a miserable business! Two are better than one because they have a good return for their work: if one falls down, his friend can help him up. But I pity the man who falls and has no one to help him up! Also, if two lay down together, they will keep warm. But how can one keep warm alone? Though one may be overpowered, two can defend themselves. A cord of three strands is not quickly broken."

Isn't it interesting that Solomon's observations about people are as true today as they were when he wrote them thousands of years ago? We may drive faster chariots today, and we may have advanced technologically, but the fundamental nature of people is the same: we need others to make our life as successful as possible.

Rob Kosberg (L) and Kevin Hutto (R) are successful business partners and great friends. They continue to seek coaching in their own lives to become more effective leaders.

This need is originally met in our lives by our parents. So many ills in our society can be traced directly back to the breakdown of the family. Unfortunately for many, they are born into circumstances that don't meet their needs physically, emotionally, or spiritually. We need the involvement of parents who love and cherish us. Studies show that even the smallest things, such as speaking to and reading to infants, stimulate their growth and development. You may look back in your life to parents who didn't seem to do much for you. It won't help you to grow bitter and angry with your parents or with God. Perhaps you can say as my wife does, "Well, I didn't get what I needed as a child and I still made it. I'm going to make sure my children or other children around me will have a better start in life than I had."

I believe that my parents, Hugh and Lillie Fuqua, raised me wonderfully. They were not perfect parents. There were things that they could have done better, but as a father figure who was responsible for his home and family, my dad was outstanding. As a mother who showed an enormous amount of love and attention to me, my mom was outstanding. If we are to develop all the skills and beliefs that need to be incorporated into successful lives, it starts with family, but it shouldn't end there. Sadly, for some, it does. They trust their family, but not many people beyond them. Your family might be wonderful, but if you are going to acquire all the experiences and wisdom you need for the life you are going to have, you will need to broaden the circle a bit. That's no judgment on your family. It's just true. You don't get to choose your family. You do get to choose your friends, influences, buddies, mates, pals, girlfriends, boyfriends, wife, husband, etc.

Many of our most influential relationships are in our lives because we choose them. Because we are influenced by our friends and others that we spend time with, we need to choose wisely. Many of us have chosen poorly when it comes to our friends. They have introduced us to all kinds of things that we would be better off having never known. First Corinthians 15:33 says, "Do not be misled. Bad company corrupts good character." A common-sense saying that I've known for years states, "If you sleep with the dogs, you wake up with fleas." All of this wisdom is saying virtually the same thing: be careful about who you allow into your life to influence you.

My parents: Hugh and Lillie Fuqua. Raised in rural Kentucky, they met on the campus of Murray State University. I learned from them that a good marriage is a team. They were an amazing one!

We live in a fallen world, and there are bad influences around each of us every day. You can't take yourself out of the worldliness of this Earth, but you certainly can decide who has an open road to your heart and mind. Sometimes in life, we get "lucky" and have a fantastic experience with a relationship that we didn't have a role in choosing. A teacher or a coach comes to mind. When that happens, praise God for looking out for you when you weren't aware of it.

Sometimes the opposite happens, and it can be really hard. It's difficult to tolerate how it feels to be under a poor leader. Truth be told, these experiences are what shape us for our future. They teach us to imitate the good and not repeat the bad. In either case, know that God is looking out for you.

Our ability to make good choices in this area of our life is crucial. This was a Fuqua family principle that we tried to teach our children from the time that they were very young. Who we have as close relationships is a huge deal and learning how to think through that for yourself is a must. I must be honest and admit that I haven't always been on target in some of my own choices. Some friendships have led to much heartache and regret. The long-term effect on my life has been difficult to live with at times. I have to balance that with the enormously gratifying long-term results of other better decisions. Let me focus on the positive and share about some of my most helpful and life-changing relationship choices.

A Trustworthy Spouse

First and foremost, among these choices, and number one by far, is my wife, Chris. Wow! What a catch she is! Now, in humility, I must say that I had help in the matter of marrying Chris. My campus minister and several friends were totally in my court trying to convince her that I was a good choice for a boyfriend and eventually a husband. We had known each other at college, but we never dated. She was interested in other guys, and I had dated other girls. I certainly had a high opinion of her, but I tended to like girls who liked me. (I know, another insecure college guy!) I am grateful for others looking out for me. I needed the help. This is an area of many young people's lives where they need a good relationship to help guide them. In matters of romance, emotions can run wild. The ramification of a poor choice here can be devastating for the rest of your life. Chris is a very talented, intelligent, and driven person. Anyone who knows us well understands that dealing with me means you are dealing with Chris. We are a team. As the Bible says, "the two become one." In many of the best marriages, this is what happens. Conversely, in many marriages that struggle for years, this is at the center of their problems. All marriages have friction from time to time, but my personal observation over the years is that the marriages that really function as "one" are the most successful. It's my business to be the leader of my house, but it's a lot easier when I can trust the judgment of my spouse, and we work as partners. Chris has had a tremendous impact on many women over the years. She is an outstanding mother to our children. She has served admirably in the ministry and also been successful in the nursing profession for years. My life may be my business, but I need Chris's help to do it right.

Trusted Friends and Advisers

Many of the presidents of the United States and other countries have had an array of hopefully wise and proven advisers around them to help with the complicated decisions that are required to be the head of government. Trusted friends and advisers can spell the difference between defeat and victory. Our history is littered with instances where bad advice led to catastrophic results and missed opportunities. Consider a world without Google in it. When it was just a startup company in Silicon Valley, someone from a rival company advised their superiors not to purchase Google for less than a million dollars. That was some BAD advice. Consider that you can buy a house (at least a small one in California) for that amount. Currently, Google is valued at more than $739 billion. Who we will listen to is a critically important decision in our lives. Who are you relying on to help you keep making positive progress in your life? Cael Sanderson, the current head wrestling coach at Penn State, an unbeaten college wrestler with four national championships and an Olympic gold medal, says this, "Unless you continually work, evolve, and innovate, you'll learn a quick and painful lesson from someone who has." The greatest athletes in the world and virtually any area of sport, even professionals, have coaches. Businessmen and women at the highest levels of business have coaches they hire for big bucks to help them stay sharp.

I have been blessed with so many of these mentors in every area of my life: marriage, parenting, ministry, recreation, health, and so on. One of the hard lessons I have learned in this area is that when someone works for you, they may or may not truly be a close friend. If your professional circumstances change, you might be in for a real wake-up call as to how close you really are to your coworkers. I am convinced that many people in positions of authority who are mentors or who manage a number of people wrongly think they have many trusted friends. In reality, they may have professional relationships that will disappear when that bond is broken.

The scriptures speak often about the close relationship that David and Jonathan had with each other. First Samuel 20:42 says, "We have sworn friendship with each other in the name of the Lord." There is a commitment implied in this text. True friends are there during the good times and the bad times. First Samuel 23:16 reads, "Jonathan went to David at Horesh and helped him find strength in God."

It certainly seems that they enjoyed each other's company, strengthened each other when they were at a down moment, and helped each other spiritually. Another passage comments that their friendship was not self-serving. Have you ever had a relationship that turned out to be about leveraging you for their own interests? That's not what true friends do. David and Jonathan evidently sensed the mutual need for friendship. If you don't feel a need for a close friend in your life, perhaps you should do a bit of soul-searching and ask yourself, "Why not?" Friendship is work. Now, in fairness, it can be pleasant work, but it is still work. If you don't spend any time with your friends, those friendships will not thrive.

When I moved to Los Angeles, one of my early coworkers was Reese Neyland. We didn't know each other at all, so I was open to whatever friendship would develop. He learned that I enjoyed playing golf, and he said, "Hey, if you are a golfer, I'm up to learning." So, we began to have many business discussions while we played a bit of golf. He is a gifted athlete, an all-American basketball player from Old Dominion University. Back in the day, they won a national championship with Reese playing shooting guard. He had a lot of natural ability to learn how to golf. At first, he wasn't very good, but over the many years, we have taken turns beating each other regularly. It started out as a business, but we have become close friends while continuing to work together as peers.

Reese Neyland, a true friend and coworker
for many years in Los Angeles.

I mention this as a great example of someone being willing to learn, to try new things and get out of their comfort zone, in order to be a friend. Sometimes we do sense that we need friends, yet we are frustrated about our lack of trusted friends. We start blaming everyone around us, including the church, the community, or our upbringing. This is a dead end. If you want to have close friends, my advice is to be the kind of friend that you wish others were. Reese was willing to go through the effort to learn a difficult sport in order to encourage friendship. What are you willing to do? Take responsibility for the state of your friendships. If you want a friend, BE a friend.

I have been blessed with so many good advisers over the years. In Chicago, we had older couples like Ben and Louise Holt and Jim and Benja Krause who helped us with our young marriage and how to adjust to being parents. Our children, Ben and Maria, were only 13 months apart, so we needed a lot of advice. (My wife Chris swears there is a three-year period of our lives that she has no memory of while our kids were both in diapers!) A business executive I knew, Cecil Wooten, took the time to help me organize our home finances. Later on, other men such as Roger Lamb and John Mannel were crucial in helping me figure out many areas of my ministry and family life. Jim Albert, Byron Parson, and Rick Berry were younger Chicago guys that were always up for discussion and a hotdog at one of the hundreds of neighborhood stands. (Yes, Chicago has the best hot dogs in America!)

My first golf group: Bob Harpole, Ryan Howard, and I played golf in all seasons, even the frigid Chicago winters, with some of the worst golf equipment one could imagine. We were poor, cold, and happy to hang out. It was an honor and one of my great joys to help build the church in Chicago and have an influence throughout the Midwest in those days. To do that, without advisers and friends, would have been a hollow experience. God put us on this Earth to work, for sure, but he also gave us each other to love, to care for, and to build family and community with. Leaving Chicago for Argentina and then moving on to Los Angeles created a whole new set of needs in my life and the need for new friends and advisers. Even in our sixties now, we *still* feel the need to have consistent time with friends who positively impact us. We meet almost every Thursday for dinner with our close friends, Rob and Connie Kosberg.

The Kosbergs and the Fuquas on one of our many outings. This was a concert featuring Journey and Santana!

We all look forward to this time together, and it's not just the food! We talk about every aspect of our personal lives—marriage, kids, work, money, and our spiritual lives. We laugh and cry together before the dessert arrives. I can't think of any topics that are off-limits for us. If we have to miss a Thursday, we fight to find another time during the week to meet. It's not because someone is forcing us to do this, but because we love it! We know it's a rare treasure to be able to support, encourage, and hopefully push each other forward in life in a great way with such trusted friends. We need this consistency in our lives, even at our age. We also need those we see less often like Mark and Connie Mancini from our college years, past coworkers like the Marutzkys, Bairds, Greens, Arthurs, Statens, and many others who have advised, guided, corrected, argued, shared meals and movies. These folks have witnessed our children grow up, and our parents pass on. Where would we be without the love, acceptance, and patience of this host of friends and advisers? I would be a mess! The successes I have had in life are in many ways—a cumulative effect of the good people God has blessed me with.

Now let's be clear: was it always easy? No. Did we always see things eye to eye? No. Relationships, my friend, are work! The scriptures say we must speak the truth in love to one another so that we will grow up and become mature and complete (Ephesians 4:15.) We all need people in our lives who love us and are willing to tell us things we *need* to hear, not necessarily what we *want* to hear. This is not a "know it all" type of friend who is regularly correcting you on all manner of things in your life. (Maybe someone specific comes to mind—that's who I try NOT to be.) Rather, it's someone who cares enough to point things out when you need it and who has your best interests at heart.

Several years ago, after a disappointing day on the golf course, Reese Neyland was complaining about how poorly he had played and intimated that maybe he shouldn't play with us anymore because he wasn't good enough. Anyone who plays golf on a regular basis has been there! Golf, even for the professionals, is a brutally difficult game. Bob Harpole asked him directly if he was practicing. He said no, he wasn't. Bob said, with no rancor in his voice, but firmly, "Either start practicing or quit griping." Boom! That was the truth, and it was said by a trusted friend. Do you know what Reese did? He started practicing on a regular basis and guess what happened—he got better and started winning! Amazing! Reese even went to a special clinic run by golf guru Dave Pelz and has developed the best short game of any of the golfers in our group.

He has a PGA teaching professional who he occasionally sees when he gets a bit off track and that resharpens his understanding and his skills. Now, we ALL wish our short game was as good as Reese's. All of this can be traced back to a trusted friend, "speaking the truth in love." Reese needed that. I need that. You need that.

Do you have people in your life that you trust at that level? When people do say things to you, do you argue, debate, minimize, turn it back on them, or do you listen? Do you have those moments in life when you feel your internal temperature rising, the hair on the back of your neck standing up, and your face blushing? Those are the "moments of truth" for us. Do yourself a favor and open your ears and heart to others who care for you.

UCLA Bruin Nation—we made each other better!

I can't leave this section without sharing about many of my former students who were converted to Christ in the campus ministry at UCLA: Rafael and Griselda Lua, Todd and Tanya Spath, John and

Lori Augustine, Darius and Suzanné Simmons, Lisa Mortimer (Holman), Francyn Herrera (Dueñas), Grace Lee (Wong), Brian Gold, Kathy Siao (Yen), Steve Hiddleson, Dave and Erin MacLeod, Larry Brent, Yvonne Lee (Lim), Kiera Wong (Vae'ena), and the list goes on. Later, Chris and I were able to spend a short time leading the University of Southern California ministry, an ironic switch for diehard Bruins fans. God allowed us to meet and enjoy so many new relationships with people like John and Arlene Markowski, Maggie Shih, Marie Agnello (Mancini), and others. These fantastic people are now bona fide grownups still solid in their faith, and many are raising their own families with college-aged children themselves. They are the next generation of strong families and singles in our church and in their communities. They are talented, intelligent, spiritual people that God gave us the blessing to lead.

One time at UCLA with the leadership group, I commented that I probably had the lowest IQ in the room. I went on to say that it wasn't important that they were academically superior to me. I was there to lead them spiritually and to teach them to pay their phone bills! We all had a good laugh! I'm very proud of my former students; they are like my children. I, myself, had the great advantage of being converted and trained in an outstanding campus ministry. In many ways, I just replicated what I experienced at EIU and adjusted it to the time and place differences of Southern California in the 1990s. People are people, and the scriptures are the scriptures. In life, we get to experience being that young guy, the middle-aged guy, and eventually, the old guy, if you live long enough. By the way, just being old doesn't make you wise. That's why the scripture in Ecclesiastes 4:13 speaks of a man being "old but foolish." Another known axiom, "There is no fool like an old fool," strongly infers that just living a long time doesn't make you wise. I am now often the oldest person in a room I'm in. I still believe I need relationships that call me higher. How about you?

Sometimes what we need in the realm of these relationships is to see someone setting a good example right in front of us. Many times, in our lives, we know what we SHOULD do, but don't follow through. Our problem is not a lack of knowledge, but our willingness to give in to laziness and selfishness. Sometimes seeing a person you trust model what you should be doing, but are not, can give you the push you need to get going. In my life, I have often been spurred on through friendly competition with my friends. A good buddy of mine, Peter Garcia, is one of those guys who sets a great example in many areas of his life. One of the areas I connect with is how he works to stay in good physical shape. In years past, I used to beat Peter in golf on a regular basis. Recently, I noticed that he was hitting his drives longer than me and often scoring better than me. We were recently at a golf getaway with our regular group and while I was relaxing in the Jacuzzi after a "long hard day," I noticed Peter was doing yoga stretches with an app on his phone. I sat there in that relaxing hot water and started thinking, "You know, maybe he is beating me because he is preparing more regularly and working harder than me." I needed a good example of a trusted friend to move me in the right direction. I don't think Pete was doing those stretches to affect me, but it did. Certainly, one of the factors of success in anyone's life is to surround yourself with those who set good examples for us, sometimes right in front of our face!

One of my most treasured pictures. Rob Kosberg (L), Peter Garcia (middle), and me at St. Andrews. We are on the 18th hole and paused on the Swilcan Bridge.

Coaches

Being a coach's son gave me a unique perspective on my own coaches. Coach's sons can tend to be hustlers and gritty hard workers, and they understand the importance of good fundamentals. They are often "gym rats" because they have hung around their fathers and probably watched them lead practice sessions and games since they can remember. My two high school wrestling coaches were Larry Kanke and Steve Durian. They were both young coaches when I came through, probably in their late twenties, if I'm guessing correctly. They were intense, focused men that were trying to establish my high school wrestling team as a powerful program in northwest Illinois. They encouraged me to go to a summer wrestling camp that had just started at the University of Iowa. The head coach there was Gary Kurdelmeier, and he had a new assistant coach named Dan Gable. Gable had just won a gold medal in the 1972 Olympics and was probably the most well-known wrestler of his time. He was, without a doubt, my hero. My mother drove me out to Iowa City and dropped me off at camp. She told me later she couldn't believe she was leaving me all by myself, all 100 pounds of me, for a week of high-powered wrestling instruction. It was scary and inspiring at the same time. It turned me into a wrestler.

My high school wrestling coaches, Steve Durian (L)
and Larry Kanke (R).

They were knowledgeable and serious coaches.
Source: JD Darnell High School

What a great job of coaching Coach Kanke and Coach Durian accomplished with my high school team. They knew I needed more, and they challenged and inspired me to do it. I don't remember a lot of negative yelling when I messed up, but lots of good teaching and positive reinforcement when I did well. My senior year, our team record was 12-4, by far the best we had ever done. After I graduated, the program became one of the elite wrestling programs in the state of Illinois. Coach Kanke's career led him to the Illinois Wrestling Coaches Hall of Fame. I needed those coaches to expect the best I could give and to challenge me to be more than I ever would have if they had not been there.

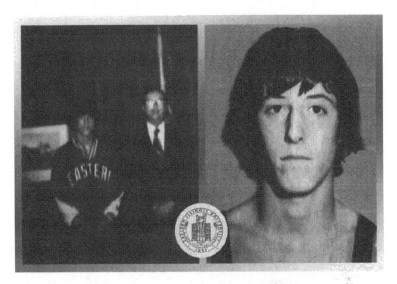

Me as a sophomore on the EIU wrestling team. The picture to the left is with my dad.

I sure wish it was a clearer picture. I wrestled in the 126 lb and 134 lb weight classes. Courtesy Eastern Illinois University

The college coach who recruited me, Hop Pinther, unfortunately, broke his back the summer before my freshman year and had to retire. In his place, the university hired a recent national champion from Oklahoma State University, Ron Clinton. He was kind of a "long-haired hippie," as my dad would have said, but was a very encouraging and energetic coach. We had a decent team—certainly not Oklahoma State, but with some really good individuals. One of them was in my weight class, Ed Becker from Miami, Florida. He had won a couple of state championships in Florida and was a really tough guy. My entire freshman year was spent being tossed around like a rag doll by Ed! Coach Clinton never yelled at me. He didn't highlight me in a negative light at all. I was discouraged. I was used to being the guy throwing someone else around in the wrestling room. I was humbled. I wasn't even close to Ed in strength, knowledge, or experience. I wondered what I had gotten myself into. Coach Clinton was nothing but positive.

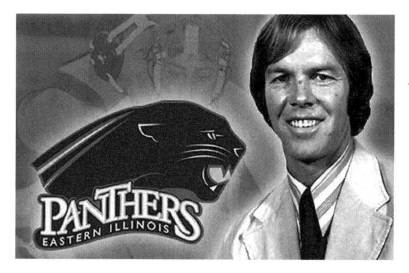

Coach Ron Clinton treated me fairly and with kindness.
Courtesy: Eastern Illinois University

The summer between my freshman and sophomore years, I lifted weights and ran like crazy. I was determined not to have that experience again. A well-known wrestling saying is, "If you are tired of getting beat, get better." My sophomore year was more successful. I wrestled some in matches, and at the end of the year, Coach Clinton awarded me a varsity letter. I was surprised. I wasn't that important to the team, at least in my eyes. I think he appreciated the fact that I didn't quit when it would have been very easy to have given up. I wasn't anywhere near the best wrestler in the program, but I came to practice every day, and I gave it my best.

This lesson proved useful when I became a Christian. My junior year, the local Church of Christ hired a man named Kip McKean to start a campus ministry. I couldn't have been less interested initially. As the Lord would have it, one of the first young men that became a Christian was my college roommate, Greg Gardner. I began going to church on a regular basis with Greg and started to see the need to get my life turned around spiritually. That created a time crunch for me with schoolwork, wrestling, and campus ministry activities. Now I'm not saying that a college student can't be an intercollegiate athlete and a solid Christian also. I have known many who were able to discipline themselves to have success on the field of athletic competition and in the classroom. But for me, it was becoming clear that I would need to choose, and the choice was obvious to me. I was very reluctant to talk to Coach Clinton, but I knew I had to. I wasn't going just to drop out and stop going to practice.

I stopped by his office and told Coach Clinton I had become a Christian and that the schedule of wrestling and campus ministry meetings was not compatible for me and that I had decided to quit wrestling. I don't know what I expected him to do, but I was so thankful and impressed by his reaction and words. He said he could tell that my mind wasn't really into wrestling for the last few weeks and that he understood my conflict. He recommended that I take the next month off from wrestling and see how I felt then. If I wanted to come back, he would be grateful to have me, but if I didn't return, he would respect my decision. He thanked me for my dedication and hard work. I was so relieved. I guess I expected him to belittle me or my faith and shame me into staying with his developing program. He didn't even come close to that. He was respectful and kind. Over the many years since that conversation, I thought of it many times. I wrote him a letter years later thanking him for his words and attitude toward a kid he really didn't need in order to build his wrestling program, but whom he had treated with respect. The team in the next few years grew strong and took second at Division II Nationals in 1979 and in 1981. In 1979 they lost first place by only one-fourth of a point. Coach Clinton went on to be the head wrestling coach at the University of Illinois. He coached six national champions and 45 All-Americans in his distinguished career.

My coaches have had a life-changing impact on me. They were tough men. They had high ambitions for their athletes and teams, and they enjoyed a high level of success. Yet, my remembrances were of their patience, kindness, and the respect they showed to me—what a lesson for any of us who are in leadership positions. You can have high expectations, be personally driven, be a person of tough character, and all the while treating people with respect! The discipline and hardline convictions that they instilled in me are a key part of me taking personal responsibility for my life.

I'll close this chapter with a story from my mother's life to illustrate how we need help from all kinds of people, including coaches and parents, to develop the character to take responsibility for our lives. My mother told me a story from her childhood that illustrates that being hard on ourselves is not a modern thing, but a human thing. Her mother, my grandmother, was named Lonnie Tennessee Steele. She married my grandfather, who was from the Eldridge family, but she was always proud of her Steele heritage. She was number 14 out of 14 kids, so I'm sure she was a bit of the baby girl of the family. Her older brothers and sisters gave her tobacco to chew on as a baby, believe it or not. They were old-time Western Kentucky tobacco farmers. Anyway, she was a real tough customer. She would remind my mother, who was also the baby of their family, when she was whining about something being too hard, "You need to toughen up and remember you are half Steele!" My son's middle name is Steele in honor of her. Sometimes we all need that reminder that we are stronger than we know. We need our family, our trusted friends, and our coaches to spur us on to do our business—the business of life. Make sure you are cultivating those crucial relationships that can be there when you need help!

Guided Reflections

1. Write down a list of 10 relationships in your life. Describe the role that each one plays and the level of involvement that you have with each.
2. What are the guiding principles that you use to select close relationships? What do you think they should be to move you in a more positive direction in your life?
3. What are three concrete changes you can make to improve your current relationships?

CHAPTER 4

It's the Little Things

The **guiding principle** of this chapter is that in considering changes that you want to make, just start somewhere. Often, we are intimidated by the amount of change that we need to make, and so we don't do anything. Pick something and change it. You will have started on a path that will lead you to even more success.

Taking personal responsibility for your life can seem like a huge undertaking. It can seem overwhelming to say, and mean, "I have got to live my life differently." Where do I start? The answer is: little things. In Song of Songs 2:15, Solomon says, "Catch for us the foxes, the little foxes that ruin the vineyards." These "little foxes" seem to be the problems that are ruining the whole vineyard. It's the "little things" that can make all the difference. It's the "little things" that begin a process that can bring about big changes in a person's life. How about a couple of good "little things" quotes? "It's the little details that are vital. Little things make big things happen." That was from the great UCLA basketball coach, John Wooden. "There are many of us that are willing to do great things for the Lord, but few of us are willing to do little things" (Dwight L. Moody). I have to wonder about many of us in this "little things" discussion. Here's what I mean. Once I start to give you the "little things" that you need to go after in your life you are going to start your normal list of reasons why these things are not that important or why they are easier for me than they are for you.

You may think this is "old school" and that I need to catch up with the modern world. (That may actually be true, but that's a different discussion altogether.) The real problem we have with the "little things" is that they are not something we do and then check off the list permanently. They are lifestyle changes. If it was for a day, we could do it! If it was for a week, or a month, we could do it. But, do this for the rest of my life? Impossible! So, essentially, we quit before making much of an effort. Our world is populated with many people who have had their medical doctor tell them, "You either change this in your life, or you will be dead in under a year." That would be a sobering moment, wouldn't it?

The things I'm suggesting here work. I know they work because I've seen them work in my life and in many people's lives around me. You have a choice. You can begin to have victory over these things in your life, or you can whine about how hard it is for you and look desperately to blame someone else for your failure. Come on; today is the first day of the rest of your life. Let's start small and have big victories in our lives! Consider these areas.

Personal discipline: I hear some of you, "Oh, boy, here we go again. Another lecture about being lazy, sloppy, and out of control." When our children were smaller and still at home, Chris would sometimes get behind the kids so I could see her and they couldn't. As I was lecturing them exhaustively, she would make a fist with one hand and smash it into her other hand and grind it in her palm. The message to me was "You are grinding them." It was a graphic communication from her to me to back off and give the kids a little space. I suppose I didn't like it when she did that, and I must say it seemed like she did it too often, but I trusted her judgment and realized that I could definitely be too much at times! I don't want to do that here. If I am a bit overly enthusiastic, bear with me. I don't want to come on too strong so as to scare anyone off, but I do have some enthusiasm about this subject. Enough said, let's get down to some good "little things."

- You need a daily schedule. Get an organizer or use your phone if that's your style. You should have things you do on a regular basis. Here are a few: Daily time of Bible reading and prayer. Exercise at least three times a week (I have run between 3 and 6 miles three times a week for decades, on Mondays, Wednesdays, Fridays.) Church on Sunday. An edifying group you are a part of on a weekly or biweekly basis. Set your alarm clock and get up when it goes off. Brush your teeth and floss daily.

- Be tidy around the house. Make your bed. Things have a place. When you use them, put them back in their place. Are you constantly saying things like, "Where are my car keys?" "Where is that flashlight?" or "Where are the batteries?" Your problem is that you use these things and set them down wherever you are at the moment, and so you have an ongoing drama in your life about who misplaced your things. Nobody else did! You did it! Things have a place, and when they are not being used, they need to be in their place. That way, you know where to go to get your keys, flashlight, or batteries.

- Be early for all of your meetings, work, church, doctor's appointments, etc. Are you late because of traffic, or are you late because you didn't leave home early enough? You know the answer, most of the time, don't you? You blame the traffic instead of taking responsibility for your disrespect of those you are meeting with. You try to laugh it off and belittle it like it's not a big deal. It *is* a big deal. It's disrespectful, and it is no way to go about your life. In the real world of business, you either get disciplined, or you are out of business. When the airline says the plane leaves at eight o'clock, you expect them to run their business in a professional and timely fashion. You build your whole business trip or vacation around an expectation that they get that plane into the air on time. Now I realize there are exceptions to this that we all understand—weather problems, mechanical problems, personal problems. But, if any of those things happen and your plane is late, they apologize and hope you will give them another chance. Maybe they even throw you a bone—something free, so you will be happier.

- Take care of your stuff. Regular maintenance items for your car, change the oil, tires, etc. If you take care of your stuff, it will generally last longer.

I hear you thinking, oh, Marty, give me a break. You don't need a break. You have been giving yourself a break for the last umpteen years. You need to start having an "inner dialogue" with yourself that goes something like this. "You lazy, self-centered knucklehead. (My dad would have loved that.) Get up and move!" Change *something*. You can't change everything that needs to change at once, but you can change *something*! I do remember hearing my dad coach football and saying, "Just hit somebody with a different color helmet. Just hit somebody!" This is not complicated. You are smart enough to know what you need to do. Having victory in this area of our lives is hard. We are always drawn to our lazy, selfish, blaming-others side. We are in a battle between our spiritual and worldly natures. In Ephesians 6:14-17, Paul uses the easily understandable example of a Roman soldier and his armor to illustrate the inner qualities that we must build up if we are to win this war for our soul. "Stand firm then, with the belt of truth buckled around your waist, with the breastplate of righteousness in place, and with your feet fitted with the readiness that comes from the gospel of peace. In addition to all this, take up the shield of faith, with which you can extinguish all the flaming arrows of the evil one. Take up the helmet of salvation and the sword of the Spirit, which is the Word of God." What are the spiritual muscles we need to exercise and make strong? This passage says truth, righteousness, readiness, faith, salvation, and the Word of God. These are six qualities of the inner person that will make a huge difference in the outer person. These are the basics, the fundamentals, the first things—the "little things" that, once incorporated into your character, lead you toward spiritual stability and maturity.

Let's just pick out one of them and expand on it: readiness. Let's plug that into how you worship on Sundays. Readiness is obviously "being ready," but it infers enthusiasm, energy, and a willing spirit. You arrive at church, and you are "ready" to be encouraging to all that you encounter, including fellow members and guests who are visiting or maybe seeking a relationship with God. When the singing starts, you sing with joy and cooperation, whether it's a song you like or a type of song you wouldn't prefer. During communion, you purposely try to focus your mind on what you are doing, remembering Jesus, and setting your mind on having a great next week. During the contribution, you are happy to give a portion of what God gave you, and you focus not on the money amount, but the priceless gifts the Lord has given you. During the sermon, you follow along in the scriptures and with the thoughts being presented by the speaker. After dismissal, you don't just rush out the door, but you visit and fellowship to encourage others to the best of your ability. You go home with a good mindset for the rest of your week. You came to church *ready*. You were *ready* for all the different components of worship. You left *ready* for a good week. You see this readiness thing is just a "little thing" that can and will turn your life around. As Coach Clinton would say while we were warming up for practice, "We are educated, motivated, and dedicated; full of devotion, emotion, and locomotion!" You could feel the energy go up in the entire wrestling room!

"Little things" can also mean what you *don't* do. In Titus 2:11-12, Paul says, "The grace of God that brings salvation has appeared to all men. It teaches us to say NO." Saying "NO" is a vital "little thing." To take responsibility for your life is not just what you say "yes" to, it is also what you say "NO" to.

Say NO to bitterness. One of the ministers who I have great respect for is Sam Laing. He once said in a sermon, "Letting bitterness live in your heart is like swallowing poison to try to harm someone else. The only person you will harm is yourself." There is not a person alive that doesn't have, at the very least in their own mind, something they can be bitter about. I find that the older I get, the more I must be on my guard against bitterness. Maybe that's because the longer you live, the more time and experiences you have that might give you a reason to be resentful. I really don't want to be a bitter old man. Not long after Chris and I were married, we were trying to resolve something, and she looked at me and said, "You are a grudger." What she was saying was that I had a hard time forgiving her when she did something to offend me. I know this is hard to imagine! Bitterness will eat you alive spiritually. Bitterness will ruin your relationships, your marriage, family, and friendships. Bitterness can destroy your church. We are all going to be "sinned against" by someone, it's inevitable. People can be real jerks sometimes. Be humbled by the truth that you can be a real jerk too. Be quick to forgive and move on.

Say NO to quitting! Finish what you start! Is your life cluttered with half-done tasks and projects? Is your garage full of household chores that you have yet to finish? There is tremendous inner satisfaction when you look at a job that you started and finished. There are many websites about this subject that you can look at and read, and they will help you. I want to approach this from the personal responsibility angle. The confidence it gives you when you finish a task will lead you toward feeling, "I can do this!" Refusing to quit until the job is done is a way to see the virtue of perseverance develop in your life. Remember, the only way to get to work on perseverance is to be tired first. Gut it out, get some input as needed, get someone to work at the task with you, and GET IT DONE!

A wonderful part of this can be to involve your children in your work. My parents had us working at something all the time—gardening, yardwork, building an addition to our house. We always had something going on. What I didn't realize until much later was how much I was learning that others didn't know because of all those completed projects. It's a bit shocking to me sometimes how many people my age don't know how to do things with their hands. They have to pay someone to do it, or it doesn't get done. I learned to work by working with my dad. I was so fortunate to have that opportunity. Moms and Dads, get your sons and daughters involved in your household tasks. Have them help you with cooking, cleaning, shopping, and decorating. I realize to some this may sound terribly "old school," but I'm not really trying to be modern or politically correct. (I'm sure that's a shock!) Obviously, there are many things that we can't do or don't have the technical training or tools to accomplish. Hire a professional, and the world goes on, of course, with you being a bit poorer! But you will be shocked at how much you can do, and what you can fix by just googling and watching instructional videos on YouTube. Remember, you are training your children to take personal responsibility for their lives, even from an early age. This doesn't have to be an awful experience that both parents and children hate. Now, to be honest, I didn't always look forward to all my parents' projects, and there were times that we didn't have fun. Sometimes it was a dirty, heavy, long day of tough work. But those project times provided some of the funniest stories of my family, and they are the stories we tell when the family meets.

There was the time when we were building a family room addition to our house, and it was my job to dig the footings so we could pour the concrete for the foundation. The contractor said they had to be 40 inches deep. After working for several hours, I told my dad that it couldn't be done by hand. My dad was concerned, so he telephoned the contractor and told him what I said. The whole project seemed impossible to me. The contractor said, "Tell Marty I have a 75-year-old man that does that on a weekly basis." To say the least, I was embarrassed, and my dad told me to get my butt out there and get the job done. We laughed about that for years. Another time my older brother Al was out in the garden pulling weeds when he noticed my dad on the back porch with his thumb up in the air and Dad seemed to be looking at him. Al said, "Dad, what are you doing?" And Dad said, "Trying to see if you are moving!" My dad thought he was so funny sometimes. We also laughed about that for years!

Say NO to ingratitude. Is there anything less attractive in a person than ingratitude? I am at a loss to know what it would be. Ungrateful children—terrible; ungrateful teenagers—deplorable; ungrateful adults—abominable. It doesn't make any difference the age or gender, ingratitude is ugly. The Lord certainly doesn't hide his disdain for it. Deuteronomy 32:6 reads, "Is this the way you repay the Lord, O foolish and unwise people? Is he not your father, your creator, who made you and formed you?" The early Christians needed to be exhorted to be happy and thankful. First Thessalonians 5:16-18 says, "Be joyful always; pray continually; give thanks in all circumstances, for this is God's will for you." It seems like a "little thing," but it really is a HUGE thing. Whether you are basically happy and grateful or whether you are unhappy and ungrateful is up to you! It is so pleasant to be around others who are grateful. They are a joy. They seem to have many friends, and they somehow look at life with zest and a smile on their face.

What kind of people do we want to work for? Grateful people. What kind of people do we want to employ? Grateful people. What kind of person do you want your wife or husband to be? Grateful! What kind of kids do you want to have? Grateful ones. Even though we know this, we have a tremendous tendency to be ungrateful and therefore grumpy, moody, complaining people who focus more on what we don't have than what we do have. We have been blessed so much. It is a good experience to periodically take out a piece of paper and a pen (I know I'm dating myself by even suggesting things like paper and pens!) and start writing down the ways we feel like we have been blessed. Counting your blessings can help you grow in gratitude and have a more positive outlook.

The simple, yet overlooked, importance of being quick to say, "thank you" to those who do things for us is huge. Our problem can be rooted in the inner feeling that we deserve to be treated well, respected, and therefore catered to. We can always find people who are in more difficult circumstances than we are in life and it is good for us to remind ourselves that, if not for the mercy of God, that's where we could be. We don't deserve health, family, possessions, abilities, a safe place to live, nor clean water and abundant food. These are blessings we have that others around the world sometimes don't have. Be grateful! Be happy! Emphasize the positive and minimize the negative. It's the "little things," my friends! The little "YES" and the little "NO" develop us into mature adults who take personal responsibility for our lives. It's *your* business!

Guided Reflections

1. What are a few of the "little things" that consistently come as challenges in your life? Choose one and create a plan to make a step to change today.

2. What do you need to say NO to quitting? bitterness? ingratitude? Create one way to show progress in this area.

CHAPTER 5

What's *Not* Your Business

Personal responsibility is, by definition, personal. It can be a big temptation for some to want not only to take care of their business but also to be far too involved in other people's business. The **guiding principle** of this chapter is to identify what is NOT your business.

As with all things about practical living, the scriptures give us some great advice. In I Thessalonians 4:11 it says, "Make it your ambition to lead a quiet life, *to mind your own business* and to work with your hands, just as we told you, so that your daily life may win the respect of outsiders and so that you will not be dependent on anybody." Mind your own business! What does that mean? I take it to mean that the quiet life, a life not cluttered with the drama of other people's lives, allows you to take care of your own life. Every life has its challenges, highs and lows, good days and bad days, losses and victories. It is a full-time job for every person to "mind their own business." This type of life is actually how God wants us to be—BUSY! Busy with the daily routine of a productive life, busy helping others, busy with all our responsibilities. When people aren't busy, they often can get into all sorts of trouble and wickedness. Remember the old saying, "*idle* hands are the devil's workshop."

It is actually very important to live a life of defined purpose. Jesus often said, "this is why I have come." He was clear about what he wanted to accomplish, what his father had sent him to do. If you don't know what you are trying to do with your life, you might feel somewhat busy. However, you may be wearing yourself out only to wake up somewhere down the road of your life and say, "What am I doing?" Remember the saying, "If you aim at nothing, you will hit it every time." So here you go, you are getting yourself organized, you have some good goals, you have good advisers, you are taking responsibility for your life and, whack, you are totally sidetracked by what's going on in someone else's life. It can be your parents, your children, your friends, your workmates, almost anyone. All of a sudden you are putting your life on pause while you immerse yourself in somebody else's drama. If only they would listen to you, they would be so much better off. Have you been there? You attempt to guide them from one drama to the next and are truly mystified as to why they don't listen to you.

This is where we have to go back to the scriptures and see that this is not a new phenomenon. This is a problem that always has been and always will be. First Timothy 5:13 talks about some distracted people: "they get into the habit of being idle and going from house to house. And not only do they become idlers but they also become gossips and busybodies, saying things they ought not to." Second Thessalonians 3:11 continues, "They are not busy; they are busybodies." It is absolutely essential for the person who wants to be responsible for their life to get busy living out *their* life, *their* dreams, and *their* ambitions. Get busy serving a needy world that needs to see Christ's love for them, demonstrated through you. The social media world that we live in is a gigantic magnet for getting embroiled in other people's business. People are constantly sharing a steady stream of information about their lives, including some things that are most likely nobody's business. If you are living in that world, you had better ask yourself some probing questions. Do you want that picture of you discussed at your next job interview? Do you want your children and grandchildren someday to ask you about that? But social media isn't really the problem, is it? They didn't have Facebook and Instagram in the New Testament era. The problem then and now was a loss of focus on doing the right things with our lives and being busy at our own business!

Gossip is perhaps one of the most overlooked sins ever! Gossip has "turned off" many people over the years to even trying to be a true Christian. They see it in the church and understandably are not impressed. You know, if one of your friends is negatively talking to you about one of your other friends, you can most likely bet that when you are not there, they are talking about you. Proverbs 20:19 puts it bluntly. "A gossip betrays confidence; so, avoid anyone who talks too much!" Leaders in the church can be and are at times, the biggest culprits in this area. Leaders, by description, are dealing with the lives of people in their area of concern. So, in a very real way, they come upon all kinds of information about people's past lives, sins, and problems. It is imperative for a leader to be trustworthy with this confidential information. Because of the nature of my job as a church leader, I can tell you for a fact that I know way more than I want to know. Keeping a confidence is part of your job as a leader. If you can't keep your mouth shut, then the ministry is not for you. If you have a reputation of not being able to be trusted, then God help your church and the people under your care. This is a very serious issue. Gossip and slander are often sins that older Christians deal with more than younger Christians.

There are times in this area of life that it is actually OK to not have an opinion on everything people may ask you. Here is the conversation: "Hey, Marty, what do you think about _____?" Answer: "I really don't have an opinion." Discussion over. You see, I'm not really supposed to have an opinion about *everything* in people's lives—it's their business, not mine. This goes to the core of why many people want to intrude into others' business. Sometimes people arrogantly believe they are smarter and more spiritual than others around them. Even if you are smarter and more spiritual than the other person, it still isn't your business to be sticking your nose into everybody's personal affairs. Mind your own business!

In this discussion, I also want to speak about parenting. Parenting is part science and part art. That means that there are things about parenting that are basically true in all cases and other things that are far more adaptable to the specific parent and child. Every parent is different, and so is every child. It can be challenging to speak of "principles of parenting" that apply accurately to all. However, I think it would be fair to say one of the goals of all parents is to raise your children in such a way so that they grow from being totally dependent on their parents to being able to take care of themselves. They should grow up. They will eventually be raised. Ideally, they go from children to adults. It is a rare case, indeed, to have a grown adult child who is still totally dependent on their parents. I would imagine in this situation that there is a fair bit of frustration with both the parents and the child. So, one of the universal goals of all parents is to raise their child from total dependency to healthy independence. I realize they are always your children. You worry about them and want to do what you can to help them on their journey of life.

My children are all out of the house and have lived mostly independent lives for many years. They still seem to "get into my wallet" some, but that's a different discussion. Parents have to think all along the continuum of their child's life, what they can be doing for themselves now that they are this old. It's normal for children to eventually learn to feed themselves, take care of their septic needs, clean themselves and the living area they inhabit, and learn to communicate with others. All of these and countless other learned behaviors should be "age appropriate." Some things naturally occur first and serve as the building blocks for future accomplishments. All children don't develop at the same rate, and that is fine. It isn't helpful to compare, but some comparison is natural and is going to happen. Here's where problems can begin for parents. Why is your child ahead of mine? What's wrong with my child? What's wrong with me? What's wrong with the school district? What's wrong with the whole system? You get the picture. You, as the parent, have determined that something is wrong and you are going to see that it gets fixed. Maybe nothing's wrong with your child, but something may be wrong with you. Your insecurities and competitive nature can turn you from a loving, caring parent into an overinvolved, overcontrolling parent.

I'm convinced that most problems that children go through in their developing and educational years will work out fine if they feel a deep sense of love and support from their parents. If your child senses your panic, they will probably feel panicked themselves. That's not to say that you shouldn't be involved in every area of your child's development. Yet, even from an early age, they should sense that you trust them to be good and to make good decisions. You should be more interested in the "behavior side" of the report card from school than you are the "grade side." When my dad would go over my report card, he made a big deal about folding under the grade side and going first to the behavioral side. My mother kept all my report cards from my grade school years, and I happened to find them recently. It was humorous and humbling to read the

81

comments from my teachers like, "Marty talks too much." "Marty needs to follow instructions better!" There were some A's and B's and a lot of C's. Not too good for me as the school administrator's kid. But I never remember feeling any sense of disappointment from my dad. He expected me to behave correctly with my teachers and classmates and to do my best. He would say, "A's, B's, and C's were acceptable but no D's! Dumb starts with D, and we don't have any dumb kids in our family." Parents can get off track when they lose sight of the process taking place that will end up with their child taking responsibility for their own life. How many people, now in their adult years, look back on their growing years and remember extreme pressure from their parents? And even though they didn't appreciate it at all, they find it tremendously difficult to stop doing the same thing to their own children. Parents, it's their life. You are day by day, week by week, month by month, year by year, molding, shaping, teaching, and encouraging the children God has blessed you with. The time that you have them at home will come and go faster than you ever could have imagined. The most important things are not their accomplishments, but the relationship that they develop with you. Help them have a sense of pride in being who they are, not insecure about who they are not in your eyes.

Growing up, I would at times (as all kids do) complain to my parents that somebody else's parents let them do things that they didn't allow. The comeback was, "Well, what's Timmy's last name?" I told my dad his last name. "Well, your name is Fuqua, and we don't do that. Your name is Fuqua, and that means something around here. We don't do something just because someone else does." People should be proud of their history, their backgrounds, and their circumstances. All that comes from parents who are molding them to be proud of who they are—who God made them to be— and proud that they have a life to live that has enormous meaning.

Parents, teach and train them to live their lives with full assurance that you love them and are proud of them. It's your job as a parent to support them. It's their job to take responsibility for their lives. There are some things in life that are just not your business. You have a lot on your plate living your own life. Demonstrate the wisdom that acknowledges acceptance of *your* role in life, which is to live your life and gladly admit that there are some things that are "not my business!"

Guided Reflections

1. Write down some areas that are "not your business" that you are drawn into. How can you set better boundaries in these situations?

2. Who would you trust to tell you that you are TOO involved in others' lives?

CHAPTER 6

The Value of Defeat and Pain in Personal Responsibility

The **guiding principle** of this chapter is that defeat and pain are a part of all of our lives. No one always wins or lives a pain-free life.

These difficult moments in our lives can teach us and provide turning points for future victories. I don't suppose I have ever met a person who enjoys losing. I've heard many over the years say how much they hate to lose. I have witnessed embarrassing behavior from both children and adults when they lose. Yet defeat is a part of all of our life experiences and can be a tremendous catalyst for true character change. I love this quote from rapper Ice-T, "Winners have to absorb losses." It is often what we do *after we lose* that determines if we are going to learn from our setback or just feel sorry for ourselves. Figuring out *why* you lost is always a great exercise. Did you prepare properly? Were you mentally and emotionally ready for the contest? Was that guy just better than you? Defeat is an important component in the lives of some amazing people.

Do you know that Abraham Lincoln was born into poverty, failed in two business ventures, was rejected for law school, had a total nervous breakdown and spent six months in bed, lost his first bid for public office (Illinois state legislature), was engaged to be married but his fiancée died, sought to be speaker of the Illinois state legislature and lost, ran for Congress and lost, ran again and won, ran for re-election and lost, ran for Senate and lost, ran for the vice presidential nomination of his party and lost getting less than 100 votes, ran for Senate again and lost, then was ultimately elected to two terms as the 16th president of the United States?

That man had more than his share of defeat in his life. When we lose, it hurts. There is pain involved. Pain can be a great educator in our lives. We experience physical pain as a protection system built into our being by our creator. We put our hand on a hot stove—ouch! We pull our hand away. We also make a note of that very unpleasant experience. Note to self: "Don't put your hand on a hot stove!" So, pain is a source of protection from further harm, and it is an educator to influence future behavior. Let's look at a few scriptures. Hebrews 12:11: "No discipline seems pleasant at the time, but painful. Later on, however, it produces a harvest of righteousness and peace for those who have been trained by it." Defeat and pain are great influences on future behavior if "we have been trained by it [discipline]." In other words, just because you lose or have pain doesn't necessarily teach you anything. But, it can, and it will, if you will let the experience inform you. You have probably heard of the "School of Hard Knocks." The idea is that you are educated by the defeat and pain you go through, and so you are smarter the next time you face similar situations.

Back in the day, my dad had a wooden paddle in his desk in his principal's office. I now have that same paddle. Believe me, you did not want to get sent to Mr. Fuqua's office for misbehaving at school.

One of his famous sayings was, "You can learn with your ears, or you can learn with your butt!" Very seldom did anyone ever get sent to see Mr. Fuqua a second time. (This is not a comment on corporal punishment, but rather an observation of the life application of his statement.) You know, all of our lives are like that: "We can learn with our ears, or we can learn with our butts." There have been many times in my life that had I only listened when people were trying to teach me things, it could have been so much easier. How about you?

When you are learning to wrestle, there are a lot of things that the coach will say not to do. Otherwise, it will lead to a bad result. One such thing was "If the guy on top has a crossbody ride on you, don't reach up and grab his head." I know this sounds technical and maybe weird to you, but just hang on. I was wrestling a really good kid from Rock Falls High School, Joe Terronez, and he let his head get a little over from where it was and what did ol' Marty do? Grab his head. Whack! I'm in a guillotine! That's a pinning hold that twists your back and painfully bends your neck. I spent most of the match trying to keep my back off the mat, and he spent that same time cranking on my neck and back. I walked around school the next day with my neck so bent that I am sure everyone thought, "What the heck happened to him?" You know, I never did that again—ever! I could have learned with my ears. Instead, I learned with my butt (neck.) Pain helps us to remember the lessons of life.

Let me go back to parenting for a moment. Parents rushing in and rescuing their kids from any defeat and pain may be robbing them of the very lessons they need. I've known parents that virtually do all of their children's homework. I know of one parent who filled out the college application and wrote the essay to get his kid into the college of their choice. She got in. Did he really help her? I certainly understand the hateful feeling it is as a parent to see our children unhappy and hurting. Yet, there are lessons to be learned in their lives, such as "You will reap what you sow" (Galatians 6:7). One of the foundational pains and motivations for becoming a Christian is being "cut to the heart"—PAIN! One of the life-changing effects of defeat and pain in our own lives is compassion for others who are hurting. We can help our children develop that most Christlike virtue by allowing them to "reap what they sow" when they do wrong. Maybe the best thing that can happen to your child is to not get the best grades in the class, to not be a starter on the team, to not have all the latest clothes or electronics. Parents, don't let your own desires for success cheat your children from the importance of learning to take responsibility for their lives.

Unfortunately, parents who overinvolve themselves in their children's lives can actually create a feeling of insecurity within them about any success they might be having. They may analyze, "Did I earn my role on the team/my grade because of me or is it because my mom or dad complained to the coach/teacher?" Parents, be involved, but let your children develop at a healthy rate and have fun. If it's not fun or meaningful for the kids, they will stop doing it as soon as they get away from you. I'm sharing from my personal example. I think I pushed Ben, Maria, and Anya too much in junior golf. I wanted it more than they did, and they all resented me for it. I had (at least in my mind) the purest of motives, and I was "looking out for them." At the end of the day, parents, your relationship is way more important than any accomplishment. If they want to do it, they will. If they don't, they eventually won't. The gracious nature of my children surely is demonstrated in that they have forgiven me for my poor judgment at that moment in their childhood. The interesting thing though, is that all three of them do have perfect golf swings! They hardly ever play, but when they do, they sure look good!

Back to our scripture

- Hebrews 12:1-3: "Therefore, since we are surrounded by such a great cloud of witnesses, let us throw off everything that hinders and the sin that so easily entangles, and let us run with perseverance the race marked out for us. Let us fix our eyes on Jesus, the author, and perfecter of our faith, who for the joy set before him endured the cross, scorning its shame, and sat down at the right hand of God. Consider him who endured such opposition from sinful man, so that you will not grow weary and lose heart."

This passage speaks to many things, but for our present discussion, let's focus on perseverance and endurance. Jesus is proposed as the role model. I suppose my first role models were my dad, my coaches or other athletes I knew, or knew of. As a minister for many years, my role model was my campus minister.

I now have many other fellow ministers who are role models to me. I think that's a pretty normal progression of life. We start out with family and broaden out to others as we age and have different interests develop in our lives. I'm convinced that having that progression and then ending up at Jesus is the best of ALL worlds. Any human, at some stage, is going to let you down because they, like you, are flawed and sinful. What a moment in life it was when you first realized that Mom and Dad aren't perfect! Unlike mere men, we can rest assured that Jesus is never going to disappoint us and that he is our ultimate and lifelong role model. He is the perfect blending of all virtues, tender as a lamb and tough as a lion. He had to endure the failures and manipulations of people around him, as we will. He persevered when he was physically tired, as we will be! He even took a nap in the middle of the day in the back of the boat! If Jesus did it, I can too! He endured through the heartbreak of seeing some close friends fail and even deny that they knew him, as we may. Apply this to any area of our lives, and Jesus lived it. Be like Jesus, and you are on the right track. Jesus even got frustrated with people around him. Could it happen to me? We are to "consider him" so that we don't grow weary and lose heart; in other words, so that we don't get tired and quit!

Understanding that defeat is a part of life is paramount in our journey of personal responsibility. We don't enjoy failures, but we endure them knowing that they will prepare us for other, and perhaps greater, challenges in our future. Pain teaches us, toughens us, and prepares us for the next hurdles of our life. Yes, defeat and pain are, to say the very least, unpleasant. They always have been, and they always will be. Sometimes they are so overwhelming we think they will kill us. We think we can't get up off the canvas another time. We probably will give some real thought to quitting. We can remember sayings like "If you start quitting, it gets easier and easier," and "Quitters don't win, and winners don't quit." You can consider the great "cloud of witnesses" who, from the other side of life and death, are possibly watching your race and saying, "Hang in there, son!" I picture my dad slamming his fist into his hand and saying, "Go get them, Mart!"

You can call to mind some inspiring quotes: Winston Churchill, when it looked very bleak for his beloved England in World War II, moved everyone with these words: "We shall go on to the end. We shall fight in France, and we shall fight on the seas and oceans, we shall fight with growing confidence and growing strength in the air. We shall defend our island, whatever the cost may be. We shall fight on the beaches; we shall fight on the landing grounds, we shall fight in the fields and in the streets, we shall fight in the hills; we shall never surrender!"

Above all, we can remember the scene of Jesus dying on Calvary—dealing with defeat and pain. The old Christian hymn authored by John Reynell Wreford, "When My Love for Christ Grows Weak," describes the scene: "There behold his agony suffered on the bitter tree; see his anguish, see his faith—love triumphant still in death. Then to life, I turn again, learning all the worth of pain. Learning all the might that lies in full self-sacrifice." God help us to take personal responsibility for our lives.

Guided Reflections

1. What was something in your life that you had to learn the hard way? Reflect on the changes that this lesson taught you.
2. What do you need to refuse to quit, even if it hurts? What are some steps you need to take to make this happen?

CHAPTER 7

This is a
Lifelong Journey

The **guiding principle** of this chapter is that the process of taking responsibility for your life is not a destination, but a journey.

Like other virtues in our lives, personal responsibility isn't something you fix that remains fixed forever. This is something in my life that I have had to learn and relearn many times. One of my observations about life is that it seems to unfold in "chapters." Chapter one—early childhood, chapter two—elementary school, etc. I find it humorous that about the time I'm beginning to understand the chapter I'm currently in, it's already time to move on to the next one! It seems I'm always catching up! Our lives are always changing. Events in the world are always changing. The financial condition of the world around us is always changing. As we age, our health can and does change. So, it naturally happens that being a person of strong personal responsibility changes as the chapters of our lives turn, like the pages of a novel. This isn't anything to be upset about. Nothing is wrong with you. Some things in life are what they are. It's not personal—it's just life. As the United States Marines' unofficial motto goes, "We must improvise, adapt, and overcome." Some things in life seem to get easier with the passage of time, but others get more difficult. We have to have a "can-do" spirit of looking at our present challenges and saying, "I'm going to improvise, adapt, and overcome in whatever comes my way."

I started running to remain in good physical shape, around 1985 around the time that my son Ben was born. I had run previously for conditioning while wrestling and I also ran cross-country my senior year in high school. I felt like it was getting a bit crazy to bulk up to play football and then cut weight to wrestle at the 112-pound class in wrestling season!

Finishing my marathon with one of my students at UCLA, Eliazar Herrera.
He helped me through the tough times on that run.

In other words, I was too small to play on the varsity football team, and I wasn't interested in being a benchwarmer. Running was my solution to this dilemma. I had not done much conditioning since my high school and college days. In 1985, I went in for my regular physical exam, and the doctor noted that my blood pressure was higher than it should have been. The doctor recommended that I start running three days a week and drink a glass of red wine on most days. In the beginning, I was exhausted running around the block! But it didn't take too long, and I was running 4 to 6 miles. I remember my first 10K in Chicago. I was so proud of myself. Later, I ran the Western Hemisphere Marathon here in Los Angeles in the early 1990s, finishing in 3 hours and 52 minutes. Since that time, I have run about 500 miles a year every year. That adds to a total of about 16,000 miles. During that journey, I have had injuries that required taking time off. I've had to learn my body and read the signs of when to push myself and when to back off. I've continued to run in almost any weather, hot or cold. I've run all over the world, thanks to the opportunities I've had to travel in connection with world missions. The only continent I have not run on is Antarctica, but I'm pretty sure I'm not going to run there any day soon!

These days I do not run as far or as fast as I used to. About two years ago, my son Ben and I went out for a run, and he kept pushing the pace. I finally stopped and said, "Son, either you are going to have to slow down, or I'll just have to meet you back at the house." I think he thoroughly enjoyed that moment! I do more "walk and run" runs now than I ever did in the past. But, I'm still out there! It's a journey, and I still have to "improvise, adapt, and overcome." After I run, I stretch and pray, leaning on a large rock wall down the street from my house. I stretch and remember Psalm 144:1-2, 5-6: "Praise be to the Lord my rock who trains my hands for war, my fingers for battle. He is my loving God and my fortress, my stronghold, and my deliverer, my shield in whom I take refuge, who subdues peoples under me. Part your heavens, Lord, and come down; touch the mountains, so that they smoke. Bring forth lightning and scatter the enemy; shoot your arrows and rout them." I pray for my family members, church situations, and thank God for keeping my body healthy enough to play golf and run. This is a privilege, not a right, and I know it.

I'm saying all of this to illustrate that anything we do for a long time in our lives is a journey, not a onetime act. There are many things like this. Our faith is a journey. Our family and marriages are journeys. The relationship a Christian has with the church is a journey. When the church is growing, and the leadership is wise and visionary, it's easy to love the church. But the reality of life is that this is not always a given. Our commitment to Christ involves loving the bride of Christ, the church, in all circumstances. Anyone who has been a Christian for more than ten years has a special place in my heart. I know that they have been around long enough to see the good, the bad, and the ugly of the church. All that being said, they are still here. Amen! "Jesus is the same yesterday and today and forever" (Hebrews 13:8); the church is NOT. This journey concept is also a great theme in the area of personal responsibility. We travel from young man to old man; single person to married person; mother to grandmother; perhaps from part of the workforce to retired. The circumstances you are dealing with are going to change, but your convictions should not. Some things are in your ability to fix if you want to fix them. Other things happen to us that we have no control over at all.

What should be a constant is the conviction that you must take responsibility for your life. People can, and often do, have strong convictions at a young age. Sometimes people look back at their teen and campus years as the strongest time in their life, as it pertains to personal responsibility. We have to be mindful of not growing old and getting soft on ourselves, thereby being a poor example for the younger generation. We will undoubtedly go through the cycle of weak to strong and back again many times on our journey. This cycle doesn't mean that you are unusual; it actually proves that you are quite human. Life calls upon us to "reboot" ourselves back to the default of the sound principles we decided upon and that are also rooted in common sense.

The concept of long-term faithfulness and reliability is highlighted in the Bible.

- The Parable of the Sower in Luke 8:11-15 reads, "This is the meaning of the parable: the seed is the word of God. Those along the path are the ones who hear, and then the devil comes and takes away the word from their hearts, so that they may not believe and be saved. Those on the rock are the ones who receive the word with joy when they hear it, but they have no root. They believe for a while, but in the time of testing they fall away. The seed that fell among the thorns stands for those who hear, but as they go on their way they are choked by life's worries, riches and pleasures, and they do not mature. But the seed on good soil stands for those with a noble and good heart, who hear the word, retain it, and by persevering produce a crop." Jesus clearly puts a supreme value on those who demonstrate being deeply rooted, those who discipline themselves from worldly worry, riches, and pleasures, and those who retain the truths of the faith and persevere to the end.
- Paul encourages Timothy to look for faithful and reliable people to raise up as leaders. Second Timothy 2:2 says, "Entrust to reliable men who will also be qualified to teach others." He also mentioned to Timothy that when selecting future elders and deacons, "they must first be tested."

Nothing is a more thorough test than the test of time. My fellow minister and former student, Rafael Lua, and his family took a family vacation a few years ago to Northern California and visited Sequoia

National Park. While there, they learned that the groves of sequoia trees grow very tall, up to 350 feet, and actually help each other by intertwining their roots into a huge root system to meet the needs of all the trees. Isn't that fascinating? They grow very tall and large, live a long time, and withstand the forces of nature because they help each other at the root level. They endure fire, drought, high winds, and floods—basically all the natural enemies of a tree—because their roots are all connected. Interestingly, they actually need fire to burn off all the small ground plants and other trees that would grow up and compete for their needed water and soil nutrients. They have to suffer through periodic "fires" in their lives to create the best circumstances to continue to grow strong and tall! If we are to make it through all that life throws at us, we are going to need similar roots. Making it to the end should absolutely be the intention of every child of God. To make it to the end, we must have roots, be connected to others who can help us, and we must persevere. Nobody gets an easy path. Everyone gets their own individual journey that is promised to be exciting, frustrating, and exhausting. Perseverance is a must.

- In Hebrews 10:35-39, the scriptures challenge us to persevere: "So, do not throw away your confidence; it will be richly rewarded. You need to persevere so that when you have done the will of God, you will receive what he has promised. For in just a very little while, he who is coming will come and will not delay, but my righteous one will live by faith. And if he shrinks back, I will not be pleased with him. But we are not of those who shrink back and are destroyed, but of those who believe and are saved."

This scripture is very much like a coach at halftime of the game, calling upon his athletes to hang in there in a hard game and not just absorb the hits from their opponent, but to get tough and take the battle to them. He is saying, "Go get 'em" and "We are not going to quit!" I urge you, on your journey toward greater personal responsibility, to hang in there. Don't quit! This is doable.

The Lua family at the Sequoias—a great lesson in how to make it to the end!
Credit: Rafael Lua

I learned something new recently about growing older and continuing to learn. Chris and I had just completed a marriage seminar for the warm and wonderful Oahu church where our close friends Saun and Anthony Galang are the leaders. Afterward, we decided to take a couple of days on the North Shore and rest. They have a championship golf course up there, and I was ready to rest and play a little golf. Well, I did play, and I played TERRIBLE! I was so disgusted with myself, the course, golf as a game, and mankind that I decided not to play the following day. Chris suggested that I was acting silly and feeling sorry for myself. I must say, I did not appreciate that analysis. As it turned out, one of the guys from church, Scotty Blaisdell, was friends with the course manager and had gone out of his way to get me a tee time for the next day. So now I was feeling burdened because Scotty had set me up to play, but I wasn't feeling like it. Chris encouraged me, and I reluctantly got back out there. The most amazing thing happened. I played one of the best rounds of my life! Here I am, not a young man, and still learning not to quit when things don't go my way. I was so happy yet embarrassed by my silly behavior. I stopped by the shop to buy a ball marker so I would have something to remember this experience. We all need reminders to be tough and to push through when we don't feel like it. Ok, that's it! Now it's up to you. What will YOU do?

The remembrance I bought at the clubhouse.

THAT'S YOUR BUSINESS!

Guided Reflections

1. What have you quit doing that you need to get going again in your life?
2. Challenge: Have an overcoming moment in your life and create a reminder of that victory.

Dedication and Epilogue

This book is dedicated to "the faithful" from DeKalb, Chicago, Los Angeles, and Moscow. We have endured and enjoyed one another over all of these many years. Special thanks to my fantastic wife, without whom I would be a mess. This is also for my children, who I adore, and for my parents, who gave me such a solid foundation upon which to build my life. I am grateful for all who had a hand in making this book a reality—Maryann Rose, Dave Lim, Rafael Lua, and the team at BSP. Special thanks to my dear friend and publisher, Rob Kosberg, who encouraged me to write a book with these words, "You have a story to tell." Thank you also to the many who inspired these thoughts and words. You know who you are!

Marty-isms

Favorite phrases on toughness, original and borrowed from those in my life.

- Progress is *always* appreciated.
- No pain, no gain.
- You can learn with your ears, or you can learn with your butt.
- Winners don't quit, and quitters don't win.
- Just fix *one* thing—you can't fix *everything*.
- Be the very best *YOU* can be.
- Try to be a part of the solution—not a part of the problem.
- Minimize the negative and maximize the positive.
- You are obligated to tell the truth—you are not obligated to tell *everything* that is true.
- No guts, no glory.
- If you start quitting, it gets easier and easier to do so.
- It takes about a year to get a year's experience.
- Quitting is NOT an option.
- If it's not broken, why fix it?

- One in a row!

- They have mastered the skill of almost saying something.

- Even a blind pig finds an acorn once in a while.

- You need to have a birthday.

- If you do the right things long enough, you will get the right results.

- It's always something.

This is me in the EIU wrestling room. Not a college wrestler anymore—but I'm still "fighting the good fight!"

Made in the USA
San Bernardino, CA
14 February 2020

64488907R00062